ADVICE FOR LIFE

THE PROJECT

Once upon a time there was a writer enjoying a warm Queensland summer day by her pool when an exciting idea popped into her head. *Let's ask my friends to share their best life advice and compile it into a book... and how wonderful would it be to publish and launch that book for my 50th birthday in May.*

It may be obvious already that writer was me, Kellie M Cox and that wonderful, exciting idea occurred randomly one sunny day in January. My special birthday coming up was in May. I'm not entirely sure I really thought that one through. But at the time of writing this page it is the Easter long weekend, which is April, and the book is at 35,000 words. If you have the printed paperback in your hands, that means together we made this project happen. Congratulations to all of us!

The idea did come about as my mind started to wonder about how to celebrate the milestone birthday of fifty. I wanted to mark the occasion and at fifty we are meant to be wise, aren't we, through if nothing more, the vast number of years walking the planet. Maybe, I secretly knew I still had much to learn and needed to call on my wonderful, creative, clinical, quirky and sometimes crazy friends to help me grow my wisdom. The project and the book, Advice For Life was born.

I have compiled the written pieces sent to me. You may notice that the formatting is different for each piece. I didn't alter the language or the formatting of the pieces. It was important to me that each piece was read in the voice of the author. My friends were given the option to choose an alias or to use their name, age, occupation or social media tags. You will see each person chose to identify themselves in different ways.

The brief was simple – write as few or as many words as you would like to contribute – write about a memorable life experience, a reflection, your greatest learning, something you would want your younger self to know or simply your best advice for life. No two pieces were alike. Each shared something unique from the author's perspective.

This was one of the most worthwhile projects I have even been a part of. I thought I knew my friends well enough, but this gave me an insight into their worlds, their values; strengths; love; fears; gratitude and wisdom in ways I never imagined possible. If anyone has contemplated such a project, I would say, absolutely, go ahead and do it. Just give yourself more than a few months to complete it.

Advice For Life has given me a deeper appreciation and respect for the amazing people that are sharing this journey of life with me. I thank each and every one of you for taking the time and putting into writing your thoughts with me and every person lucky enough to stumble on this little book of ours.

School really affected my confidence. Before going to school, I was a pretty confident kid. I remember one day I was ejected from choir. I was told my singing wasn't good enough and was forced to wait in the hallway while the other kids got to enjoy the practice.

When I was asked to write for Advice For Life, I told Kellie that I couldn't write as I am a terrible writer. I told her about the day in school my English teacher, Mister C, looked over my essay and told me it was *horrid*. I remember the exact word he used to describe my creative writing…*horrid*. He went on to even say that my handwriting was terrible. The writing he said was too small to read. I have never again written, until now.

Margaret Cox, age 81.

But look at you now Mum, at 81 years of age… your writing is
featured in a book.
You are a published writer!
Kellie

LOVE IN ALL ITS FORMS

Let's start with my favourite of all topics… Love. I love love! I love falling in love, I do it often. I fall in love with friend's fur babies. I fall in love with a song, a scent, a sunrise. I fall in love with a city (more cities than I should really admit to.) Love takes so many forms.

I have worked in the field of psychology/counselling for more than twenty-five years and have been in the privileged position to hear many stories of love. When clients speak of love lost and life shattering heartbreak, there is one ideal that I like to share. The symbolic representation of love in our bodies is our heart and the heart is a muscle isn't it. It is actually defined as a muscular organ. What do we know about muscles? If not used muscles waste away but if flexed, if used, trained and pushed they get stronger don't they. What happens to us when we allow love into our lives, into our bodies? We get better at it. We get better at loving others and most importantly loving ourselves.

Some clients have shared that they feel they will never stop loving the one they are grieving for and I wonder why we try? Maybe for each person, each place, each moment that we fall in love with, a tiny little piece of that love embeds itself in our heart. It got in there somehow didn't it, so why do we work so hard to try to remove it? Maybe it sits there forever. Maybe it is what makes our heart stronger. And the interesting thing is, once you have loved, truly loved, even if it wasn't a forever love, doesn't that prove that you are capable of the great and all-powerful emotion. If we have loved once, we know we can love again.

This crazy thing called love, also has another incredible quality. It is endless. It really is. There is no limit to the amount of love we have today, tomorrow, even next year. We cannot possibly run short of love. It somehow magically conjures into a whole fresh new batch of sweet, intoxicating and magical wonderment. I haven't shared this out loud before, but I feared I would never be able to love my youngest fur baby as much as I should. I already had my beautiful six-year-old German Shepherd girl, Rose Jasmine Petal when we brought Geoffrey George Michael into the family. I had loved Rose for six years already, she was my best friend and this second dog, sure I would grow fond of him, I was certain, but I could never love him as much as I loved Rose.

Well, if you have met Geoffrey George Michael, you would understand that from the moment he stepped into our lives, there was just an overwhelming feeling of love for the little guy. That didn't replace my love for Rose, nor was it even the same. He was his own person, his own little character who you couldn't help but love. Love has no limits. We can conjure up as much as we need.

There is also no limit to the number of times we can tell someone we love them. I try to say it often. It isn't always returned but that's ok. It is more important for me to say it than to have the sentiment returned. I often tell my friends; I love them to bits. I share it in texts, and emails as well. I am always posting about the amazing people I love so much. There is a reason behind all the love chatter. It comes back to the last words I ever said to my father.

My father was just an incredible loving man. We lost him over a decade ago now. Much time has passed but what hasn't passed is the vividness of the last time I saw him. He was in a hospital bed. My sons were with me. My mother was beside my father caring for him. He had survived the cancer that was threatening his life for over ten years. He was a fighter, that's for sure. We had many occasions over those years where we thought we would lose him and each time, he kept recovering, leaving hospital and hanging around for yet another Christmas and State of Origin series. Go Queensland!

This final day didn't feel all that different to the next. I had planned a camping trip for the boys and went in to see Dad before we went away. I said to him as we were leaving, "See you after the weekend." He looked straight at me, pursed his lips and shook his head ever so slightly. I knew exactly what he was telling me. He was telling me he was not going to last the weekend. I wanted to cancel the trip, to stay beside him. I didn't want to leave, but he was insistent. He told the boys he loved them and gave them one final instruction, "Look after your mother!"

He looked to me and said, "I love you." I told him, "I love you" back and we left. I made it the down the hallway of the hospital and into the lift. I couldn't contain it a second longer and broke down right there in the elevator. My poor kids didn't know what to think. I couldn't even speak. I knew it was the last time I would see my father alive. It was hardly believable that he could go from sitting up in bed, giving his final instructions to all, as the bossy father and grandfather he had always been, to dying just a couple of days later. But he did, he died, just as he knew he would, but the final words spoken between us, were the three most important words of all… I love you!

So, when I tell my friends and family, I love them. I never do it lightly. I do it because out of all the things I want you to remember about me, is how very special you are to me and how much I love you.

Enough from me, it's time to hear what some of my friends wrote about love in all its forms.

Kellie M Cox

BE YOUR OWN BEST LOVER (and I don't mean masturbation though that could be part of it).

Love is a verb, a doing word. We know from an early age that we are loved, by the things people do for us. Saying "I love you" is empty without the actions that demonstrate the truth of that. If the saying "you can't love someone else until you love yourself" is true (and I think it is) then you need to be loving yourself in all your actions. Think about what you would want a lover to do for you and do that for yourself. Make sure the things you tell yourself are kind and caring, be gentle with yourself, cook yourself nice nutritious food, be generous with yourself, do things you enjoy that make you laugh...be your own best lover!

If you aren't in a relationship, this will set you up to attract someone who behaves toward you in a similar way and if you are in a relationship, it will enhance it because you are going to be able to love your partner more deeply.

Deb, age 70.

I came to this realisation after I broke up with someone I deeply loved.

Grief is the shadow of love. We cannot grieve for something we don't care for. To wish for a life without grief is to wish for a life where you will never love. No thanks. Give me a chance to grieve and I know I've experienced love.

Craig Merriman

While reflecting on my past struggles it got me to thinking. What really resonated to me was how I had retained insecurities about not being chosen.

There is nothing better than being chosen. Chosen by the person you love, chosen by friends and loved ones, chosen for you – the amazing and fabulous person you are. To be chosen by someone you also choose is the dream. The most wanted end goal. To feel safe.

Feelings are scary things. It takes a person really secure in themselves to open up completely to another person. To be honest and transparent. To be unconditional requires immense courage. Many aren't sure of how to communicate their feelings or aren't willing to jump into a deeper level of emotion because of fear. Fear can be an enabler to your success or failure in life and love. I think we need to be a little bit scared but display bravery and also take a chance. So many facets of our fears can manifest in our inner insecurities.

Forever questions of do they find me attractive? Do they enjoy my company? Do they love or even like me? The ruminations of doubt…It is deafening in your mind. Waking next to someone new and hoping tomorrow will be enjoyable and not awkward. Hoping to discover some joint interests and common ground.

It's so empowering to have the gift of choice, but to be chosen by someone is something special.

Knowing that someone has picked you out of the many billion people on this earth to be their person, is an incredible thing. They have done this, no need for doubts and questions, no one else to blame, they chose you, all by themselves. The excitement, elation, love and security within your relationship is set on a beautiful foundation of mutual love.

The gift of choice is an amazing luxury we have, but something I do not take for granted.
As my friend, I choose you…

You appeared just at the right moment in my life, and you've stuck around through thick and thin.

I thank the universe every single day that our paths crossed because you've accepted me, loved me and helped me unconditionally.

You warm people's hearts whenever they're around you.

You make every person around you feel better. You're the first person to lift everyone up and ask for nothing in return.

And even if you are the worst at returning my calls and messages, thank you for entering my life. Thank you for learning about me and showing me the most sincere support and unconditional love.

I choose you too…

"The wings of Angels are often found on the backs of the least likely people"

Rick (aka Lord Rickster)

When the rain falls, I hold you.
When the sun shines, I bask in you.
When the moon is high, I dream of you.
When the dawn breaks, I make love to you.
Always in my heart I am one with you.

Kellie M Cox

Get a Dog and Get a Life

Seriously.
There is no greater unconditional love or loyal companionship than that of a furry four-legged canine.

They're devoted. You can walk out to check the mail, and they will be waiting at the front door to greet you like you've taken a long trip to Paris and been gone for a decade!

They're accepting. They love you for just being you. They don't notice your flaws or mistakes and to them you are their world. They will listen to you without interruption and without judgement. They don't care if you're rich or poor, short or tall, young or old.

They're helpful. Yep, you drop food, they'll clean it up! No more vacuum cleaners necessary. They're that good. If you're so inclined, they may even rinse your dishes before you load them into the dishwasher. They help you dig holes and are perfect little landscapers, letting you know the perfect place to plant a tree! They're great at those little jobs!

They're selfless. They will let YOU choose what you want to watch on the television without wanting the remote to channel surf, and they're the best at snuggling on the couch too! They only want to give love and receive it in return.

They're protective. They function as security systems and their natural instinct is to protect you. Even small dogs will alert you to unfamiliar people and noises, and there is no bolder dog than one who wants to protect its family.

They're grateful. Well, most of the time! They will eat almost anything you put on their plate without complaining!

They're adventurous. Even a trip down the same street for the umpteenth time is so exciting, but if you want to discover somewhere new, your best exploring buddy is your dog.

They're inspiring. They make you stop and smell the roses. Literally. When Rover is smelling the grass, you have to stop to smell the roses too. Think about that one. That's important.

They're humorous. They will give you something to smile about every.single.day. Yes, truly. It might be tongue kisses, desired or not, invited or not. It might be watching them splooting, yes that's a thing. Or it might be watching them racing like a lunatic around the house after a bath. There are many reasons to laugh at and with your dog. And that means…

They're good for your health. Yes, we know laughter is good for the soul. We know laughter is the best medicine because it reduces stress and anxiety, lowering our blood pressure and therefore it may protect you from heart disease.

They're sensitive. They know when you are sad, and they will do anything to cheer you up, from grabbing their favourite toy to share with you, to licking your tears, to just being by your side. They offer constant cuddles, so you don't feel socially isolated, and they reduce loneliness.

They're matchmakers. Whether you're after a life partner or a friend, just like in the Disney movies, your pooch will introduce you to others. They cannot help but socialise with dogs, and by sheer force you will be making friends with their owners – like it or not.

They're great teachers. They will teach you to be patient, to appreciate the small things in life, to embrace happiness, and that you are accepted truly and fully. If you are looking at parenthood, a dog will teach you compromise with your partner as you navigate responsibilities. A dog will teach your children love and empathy.

Getting a dog gives you a more fulfilling life!
And while your partners and children, friends and family may break your hearts many times, a dog will only break your heart once …. the day they leave you with only memories when they depart for the rainbow bridge.

Nadeyn Bryant, Practice Manager, age 50.

Magical Muses

I smell you…you are the delicious marriage of rich coffee and buttery pastries. Your aroma saturates my home and ignites my senses. You are delicate but powerful, dark, strong and intense. You start my mornings and end my nights. You are forever on my mind.

I hear you…you are the words I longed to resonate with since I dreamt of becoming your queen. You are faithful, loyal and loving. You tell me every truth I wished for. You will forever be the one truly benevolent being in my world.

I taste you…and you taste me. Your teeth rip through my skin and pierce my soul. You bring me to life with the passion that becomes of the evolved being. I am forever in your debt for making me feel again. My body responds to your tantalising mouth on mine. I will always yearn for you.

I see you…and for the first time someone sees me. And it is you. My soulmate. Your smile, your skin, your words on paper. I see the marks you make on the world and on me. I find inspiration from the vision that you share. When we are together, I am home.

I touch you…you reach through me and take my heart for you know now and forever it belongs to only you. You squeeze gently on the delicate organ. A mere touch that stimulates every other sense within me. You know your power and you use it wisely. I feel you with my core. You are my one true love. I will die with you, for without you, I would not have lived at all.

Kellie M Cox

When you find YOUR person, show them you love them
every day. I do!

**Rose Jasmine Petal, most beautiful German Shepherd in
the world, age 10.**

GO BIG AND THEN GO HOME!

I borrowed this line from the written piece by two inspiring action/adventure lovers who kindly contributed to this book. This line says to me that there isn't always the black and white in each option. It is not that we have to choose between going big or going home, that another option is possible. You do your best, strive your hardest, survive the unthinkable and then you get to go home, to rest, to recover, to replenish. And in thinking that, doesn't that lead to the idea that going big is as big or as little as you want.

My idea of going big is not going to be the same as the person next to me. It certainly is nowhere as big as the two adventurers in the story. Maybe going big is just going beyond what we imagined possible. In my clinical work, I support a lot of clients with anxiety. Once we have established rapport and trust and determined their goals to achieve in counselling, I often set them a specific homework task. It is to do one thing each day that scares them.

This can be as small or as large as the client is capable of. For one person, it might be as simple as trying a new food or saying hello to the barista making their coffee. It could be much larger, as in taking a different route home, potentially getting lost, joining a new group or taking a new class. Sometimes, my clients surprise me, they leave the counselling space, inspired and encouraged and go straight out and overcome their greatest fear. Often, they start small and work their way up to the bigger conversations and the greatest challenges that they want to achieve.

Think about what it would be like to do something each day that scares you. If you imagined now, what would the first thing be? Maybe starting small is easiest for most people. Imagine if you did this each day, found during the course of daily life one opportunity each day to extend yourself. One task faced that you would normally avoid. That could be as simple as smiling at someone, saying hello, going outside, reaching out to someone, experiencing something you have always wondered about and been too scared to try. Imagine if the next day and the next day after that you found one, just one thing to do that you would normally avoid due to fear, stress or anxiety.

Do you know what eventually happens? You run out of things to be fearful of. The fear is in the anticipation of the event. For trying that new food, you imagine what it might smell like, what the taste or texture would be like. But the moment you take that first bite, the fear has gone, because you are no longer wondering, imagining the worst most disgusting features of the food. Instead, you are knowing. You don't fear the unknown, you have made the unknown familiar. You may never try that food again. Your assumptions may have been entirely correct, and that item was never going to be a delight to your palate, but you have removed all reason to fear it.

This may sound like the simplest of techniques but give it a try. Try it for a month and even after just 30 days, you may surprise yourself with the number of stresses you have removed from your life. For the price of this book, I bet you didn't imagine you would get free therapy, but there you go. Hope you give it a try.

My courageous friends and family shared some wise words about striving to do better, be better and challenge themselves in ways which I hope you all enjoy reading.

Kellie M Cox

I used to believe that any sentence with the word "can't" had an opposite, and it was almost always a negative one. "I can't fly" well maybe not in the strictest sense but you can get on a plane, or a helicopter, or in one of those wing suits and if that doesn't suffice then the solution might be found in taking a step back in your thinking. What are you trying to achieve that you think is only possible by flying? Are you trying to traverse a great distance? Great, take a boat or a train, drive there. Do you want to feel the wind in your hair? Climb a bridge, or hike to the top of a mountain. Do you want to feel free? Well then take a good hard look at your life and figure out what is making you feel anything less than free, I can guarantee you it's not your inability to sprout wings and fly around.

There are an infinite number of things we can do at any moment of any day, but we are so quick to accept the world as a series of yes/no options because it is easier to comprehend that way. Often times we use the word can't to excuse us from doing things we don't want to do. "I can't go out with you tonight, I have work tomorrow." Well, you can, but then you would be tired and underperform at work. The much less appropriate truth is that "I can go out with you, but I don't want to or rather that there are things that I want more than to go out with you, like feel rested in the morning."

You can win that race, or fly, or go out with that person but doing so requires effort, which most of the time would be better spent elsewhere, and that's a very reasonable opinion to have, but it should not be confused with our inability to do so.

Connor Renwick

In this world of competition, I decided a few years ago that I was going to be "better today than I was yesterday" … of course this means at least a few things:

- That I am not happy with Status Quo, I want more. But this means I want more from Me, not anyone else. Learning is my journey and therefore I continue.
- But it also means that since I don't compete to be better than others, I don't see myself superior to anyone. And most certainly not inferior. I never saw myself as such…from anyone.
- I dislike my own limitations, so I strive to conquer them…you want to see my happy? Teach me something.

Vasco Vellez, Entrepreneur and Trail Blazer.

From Oars, Finding Awe
20 Lessons Learned on the River

It's amazing how an experience can stay with you forever, even when the memory seemingly fades. It's only been four weeks since we were on the raft and already the vivid color of the canyon is fading from my mind's eye faster than the silty riverbank's sand had slipped through my fingers.

The feeling of the blazing sun on my skin is disappearing just as quickly as my tan! This is why we write...to hold onto the little moments. If not documented, they run the risk of being lost forever in the day-to-day mundanity of life and magical sunsets are taken over by shopping lists and to dos. We learn so much about ourselves from travel. We gain insight from others and situations we would otherwise never be in if we were to stay safe in our little home bubble. The canyon is definitely one of those places where there is a lot to be learned.

It started at 7am on our first day when we pulled into the Moab Adventure Center car park. There was a familiar feeling; anticipation, like it was the first day of school. 16 Strangers stood in their small groups, cautiously watching each newcomer arrive. Not sure; what to do, where to stand, just waiting for the next direction and anxious to begin our adventure. At that moment, none of us knew that at the end of the next four days, these 16 strangers would become great friends.

DAY 1

The put in was a few miles downstream from Moab; we clambered aboard what would be our home for the next 4 days, not knowing what was ahead but more than ready to embrace the adventure. One thing was for sure, the scenery was spectacular, right from the start! Sounds were of the calm waters, gently lapping against the boats, and the burble of the boat's motor, punctuated by the flap of the American flag in the breeze. The first day provided ample time for floating along, spotting many cliff granaries from the ancient Anasazi Indian culture. Our river guides; (Carter, Jon and Taylor) imparted their extensive knowledge in what we'd come to call "GEE WIZ Moments"... and there were plenty of opportunities to jump into the river to cool off under the crayon-coloured canyon sun. These opportunities weren't just to take in the scenery, but also for what was fondly known as "smile breaks" (where you'd wade into the water and smile (AKA: pee breaks)!

LESSON LEARNED: "Only pee in the river. NEVER on the land"

LESSON LEARNED: "Be mindful on your "smile" breaks of those who are downstream from you!"

We awkwardly got our sea legs as we moved about the boats, getting to know our fellow travellers; The Brit family; Ian, Jacqui, their daughter Kat and son Dan... The Americans; Jeff and Traci (from Portland, Oregon), Ryan and Renee (from Reno), Kent and Desiree (from L.A. California), Bob and Peg (formerly from Atlanta, now NYC) and Jason and Steph (from New Hampshire) and us (the two token Aussies!) Lisa and Tani....Together we formed a motley crew of 16, and 3 guides, taking various forms of captaincy.

LESSON LEARNED: "The faster you get to know people, the more fun you'll have".

"I've never truly understood the word "AWESOME", until now". Subsequently it forced me to reconsider my vocabulary! Now I fully understand what the word means. I am in AWE, and to this end, my words fail me. Thank god for cameras! Even then, I do not think its beauty would be done justice. Never have I felt so small! The canyons towered above us like stone giants as we gently cruised along the river. The water, on this day, was calm and slow; I marvelled at how it has travelled so far to arrive here. From being snow on top of mountains miles away, to transforming structure, becoming water and trickling to us at that moment. It was hard to believe that this gentle, docile body of water would soon become raging rapids.

We were told that Cataract Canyon, in spectacular Canyonlands National Park, offers a YinYang combination of relaxed floating and exciting whitewater rafting. We gazed at its scenery and enjoyed delicious meals prepared by the fellas. There were "GEE WIZ" moments; including a short hike where we learned about pictoglyphs and pectoglyphs...and by about 4pm, we pulled over to begin setting up camp and we became acquainted with "fire lines" to get all the gear off the rafts.

LESSON LEARNED: "Working as a team, makes the work easier!"

We watched the boys play soccer while the sun was slowly setting. They kicked the ball in the soft, dusty sand, creating a haze around them. It's not just the awe-inspiring sights that make this place so magical, it's the sounds of everything around you; That night the air was full of the sounds of conversation and laughter; the birds, bugs and the river were a symphony of nature. The sun sets very late compared to Australia and from 7:30 it was not even close to dark. Shafts of light fingered over the top of the canyon, creating stunning pointers against the brilliant blue sky. The wind was still warm, like a cuddle, blowing away the dry heat of the day. As it became darker, the same trees that under the midday sun looked dull grey/green ghosts totally transforming apparent natures. Bursting alive with the sounds of insects and birds, the canyon had woken up, just as we lay down to sleep!

Everyone in our group declined a tent, opting instead to just sleep in the cots, using the stars above as the ideal rooftop. Blanketed in stars, we felt the romance of open air, until a crack of thunder in the distance and a lightning storm tormented nearby! Only one in our group ended up erecting their tent that night, and it made me realise, I think I'm starting to get better at not worrying so much about the things I can't control. The old me would see storm clouds and freak out about flash flooding! But now I just listen to the water lap against the bank and watch the clouds roll through and the lightning strike. What will be, will be. Mother nature smiled on us this night, and kept us from the rain, while entertaining us with a phenomenal lightning show!

LESSON LEARNED: The Yin & Yang force of nature. At times incredibly peaceful and other times, powerfully fierce.

DAY 2

Waking up in the canyon is like waking up on Mars! You're surrounded by high walls of Jurassic stone and as the sun rises, a beautiful array of colour starts to appear; reds, orange and pinks paint across the towering walls. Inch by inch making its way, until the canyon is aglow. I watched the camp as people started to stir in their sleeping bags. A new day had begun, and a new adventure awaited us!

Coffee was brewed at 6:30am, with a fresh breakfast on the plates by 7, accompanied by a holler from the guides - "Come 'nd get it!". Spoons and forks were quickly replaced by bags and firelines and we were almost ready to go. Before one last visit to a room with a view (the toilet)! This is the most adventurous thing I had done so far on this trip (aside from skydiving!). That toilet was something else! You might think it would be sleeping outside, with nothing but a cot and sleeping bag, under a lightning storm...but no, taking a poop.
LESSON LEARNED: The last thing in camp to be packed up each morning was the toilet...and we were told, "Groove before the last call!"

The raft awaited us and soon we were floating down the river about a mile, preparing for an upcoming hike. By lucky chance, Jon (the guide), was a trail runner, and when he offered to take a handful of us for a run up the canyon wall, we jumped at the opportunity. Jon was like a mountain goat, easily jogging up the face of the mountain side, wearing flip flops, and making it look easy! We weren't far behind him for about halfway, then, sheer steps slowed us down to a walk. By the time we reached the top, we were wheezing, panting and coughing. The dry, dusty mountain air choking in our throats, chests heaving...and Jon didn't even break a sweat! Arriving at the summit, we were rewarded with a stunning view of the river, being able to see it snake its way around the big sweeping bend in the canyon. Here there were photo opportunities, but some a little too close to the edge for my wifey's liking!!

There was a chin up rock, where the competitive few amongst us did a few pull ups, only to be "shown how it's done" by Jon, who managed 23 before even looking like slowing down! This section of the Colorado runs through beautiful red rock canyons. There was wildlife, including; great blue herons, squirrels, ducks and deer. Summer days can be scorching hot, and there is little shade along the river. We took brief opportunities to huddle under beach umbrellas that the guides would erect at lunchtimes and also dunk ourselves in the refreshingly cool river.
LESSON LEARNED: "Sunscreen is your friend....and 15+ isn't going to cut it, and neither is 1 bottle for 4 days!" (Thanks Brit. family for sharing yours!)

The white water begins 4 miles downstream from the confluence of the Green and Colorado Rivers, deep within Canyonlands National Park. From here, 31 rapids lay ahead. Many class 3, 4 and several class 5, with names like; "Hell to Pay", "Little Niagra" and "Satan's Gut". That gave us a wild ride before we'd reach the quiet waters of Lake Powell.

Our plan was to "Go big, AND THEN go home!"
To make our way through the rapids, we had the choice of 3 fine vessels...We named them as follows:
RAPID FIRE! = The oar / paddling boat, where you were expected to "Paddle deep and paddle hard!" plus trust in our river guide, (Carter) to navigate and tell us when and what to do.
GREEN MONSTER = The rowboat, where Jon did all the rowing work, but you were still very much in the white-water action.
BABY BULUGA = The S-Rig / A big, motorised boat, where you could cruise like Queen of the Nile!
We were told by Carter, "There are two ways we can make it through these rapids: swim, or paddle...and I prefer to paddle!" Though interestingly, Carter was the first of the group to fall overboard! He'll deny it happened, or maybe suggest that he was demonstrating to us what to do when someone falls out?! In any case, it was probably good practice, because on only Rapid 5, we lost 6/10 of the people in our boat!
LESSON LEARNED: "First rule of the river = stay in the boat. Second rule of the river = Refer to rule 1. STAY IN THE BOAT! Third rule of the river = Trust your guide."

We ran 11 rapids on day 2, highlights of which were;
- Carter going overboard at Spanish Bottom (not even technically a rapid!!)
- Rapid 5, where we lost 6 people overboard in the paddle boat
- Rapid 10, where Peg fell out
We gained more confidence, with each rapid...becoming a well-oiled paddling machine!!
LESSON LEARNED: "You can't quit halfway through; you've got to finish on the river".
LESSON LEARNED: "You've got to roll with the punches. Things happen, and you'll deal...and you'll be okay".

LESSON LEARNED: Redefine your definition of "You're Okay". "You can be tired and scared, and you're still okay!... Unless you are in need of urgent medical attention – you're okay!"
LESSON LEARNED: "You might learn your limitations will most surely push your comfort zone, from; running category 5 rapids, to bathing in the river"

We embraced canyon life with all our senses; being unplugged; no comms, and no distractions! The Brit. Family said that it was the BEST family bonding experience and that they'll never forget these moments! There's something special about watching a father and daughter sitting side by side, with no phones, just real conversation.
In the afternoon we all enjoyed a laugh and chatter was easy as we sat half submerged in our camping chairs, waist deep in canyon water. We found space on the riverbank to set up our cots for the night and bathe in the river... One of the ladies in our group said to me, "Shampooing hair in a dirty river is still better than not shampooing at all". But I don't know, as I never did it. I can tell you that when I'd shake my head, sand fell out! But that's Canyon life!
LESSON LEARNED: We don't really need all those girly products!

Later, in the evening, guitars came out and we learned that life is indeed better with a guitar and people like Jon and Taylor who know how to play it and we all enjoyed a sing a long...
We got treated to 3 shows that night! 1)The guitar/sing a long 2) The stars /meteor shower 3) Flight of the micro bats (in their hundreds, who swooping and dived). Some would say that the best show of all was watching Renee or Desiree do a dance/squeal /flail about in their sleeping bags as a micro bat got a little too close for comfort! They were super effective at driving away the May flies though!

DAY 3
The daily rituals of canyon life were starting to feel comfortable. The caffeine addicts, waited eagerly by the cowboy coffee pot, empty cup in hand... Ian, Ryan and myself (Lisa) were always first there. This day, the river courses through 20 more of the biggest rapids of the trip, including; Hell to Pay, Panic Button, Ben Hurt, Big Drop 1 and 2, Satan's Gut (where those who were in the paddle/oar boat learned a group move called "ALL IN" to get through one of the most technical rapids), Powell's Pocket Watch, Repeat Rapid, Ten Cent, Imperial

Rapid, Waterhole (where Stefanie and Jason went for a swim) and Crabby Night.

We were treated to more spectacular canyon walls and in between all the exhilaration we pulled off onto sandy beaches for meals. Let me tell you about these meals, not a tinned product in sight! We dined on marinated chicken breast with a strawberry and balsamic salad, grilled salmon fillets, succulent steaks and tasty taters. Desserts (which were well earned) were chocolate cake with vanilla frosting and vanilla cake with chocolate frosting - cooked damper style (may have also had a bit for breakfast the next morning...but maybe that was just me?!), scrumptious cherry and peach cobblers and caramelised banana and ice-cream. This really turned our camping into "glamping."

With 31 rapids now behind us, we lazily floated to our last overnight camp. Baby Beluga beached herself on a beautiful secluded sandy beach. It was 3 o'clock in the afternoon and the sand was still blisteringly hot after baking in the sun all day. We hopped, stepped and jumped our way over the scorching sand, dropped our bags, then quickly retreated to bathe our bodies in the reprieve of the cool river water.

Enjoying the last moments of daylight; chatting, laughing and watching the boys (and Tani) be boys; showing their feats of manliness by hauling large rocks from the canyon walls, down to the river. Then they'd carry their rock, underwater, for as long as they could walk out... There was one slight moment where we thought we'd lost Ian. Just turns out, he's really good at holding his breath! No lives were lost on the river that day!

That evening was a special event: "The Captains Dinner" where our river Captains/guides said that they would wear black tie attire and formerly serve us dinner, and that we should also dress to impress in our best. Our attire was to be created from our bed sheets, and our group didn't disappoint! This creative group of people fashioned everything from; sumo diapers, to Grecian draped dresses, to turban headwear and even an especially notable backless AND bottomless look that Desiree modeled as she walked through camp, that I think we'll all remember!!

After dinner, with bellies full and content, we had another kombayah moment, where the boys brought out the guitars; this time treating us to original lyrics. We sang, sat, listened and reflected as Carter read poetry by torchlight about the river we'd come to feel connected to. The sun doesn't go down till about 9pm, and it was a struggle to keep our eyes open long enough to see the billions of stars overhead. We did our best to soak up every last moment, knowing that when we awoke, tomorrow we'd have our last day together.

DAY 4

We cruised the final hours on the river, literally in flow between raft and mindset. We would occasionally jump overboard and bob along next to the S-rig. In the water you start to feel a part of and connected to the canyon and with nature. Like you've always been there and a part of you will always remain.

By midday we were starting to see what looked like civilisation again, in the form of the John Lesley Powell Bridge. I think we were all a bit sad to see it, because it meant goodbye to canyonlife and we knew that after lunch we'd be bidding our guides farewell too. Our river guides; Taylor, Jon and Carter were kind, thoughtful, friendly and professional. They were a huge part of our magical experience and will always have a special place in our hearts.

After saying goodbye to the fellas, we waited. As airports go, this is the most scenic airport gate I've ever seen! For the first time, we were looking down on the canyon rather than up. We were back up top...and about to get higher. As we watched, three small Cessna planes approached from the distance and landed on the world's smallest air strip! These 3 planes, flew us all out in groups of about 6 per plane, back to Moab, Utah. Our pilot casually mentioning that these planes were built in the 70's did nothing to ease my wife's flying anxiety!!!

I heard a range or stories from those in the other planes about their experience on the flight out. They ranged from, "The pilot was more interested in swatting a wasp that was in the cabin than flying the plane!"... to... "Poor Dan (aged 9), filled 4 bags with sick!". In my plane, I heard the female voice of the pilot in another plane asking my pilot, "Where are you?!" (again, not confidence instilling!) but, after

40 minutes in the air, we did make it safe and sound to our destination. Desiree's fingers may never be the same, after enduring Tani's vice-like grip for most of the journey!

The bus trip from that landing strip back to the compound where our cars were being held was reflective for most of us. And back at the cars, we said our goodbyes. There were warm hugs and promises to stay in touch. As the days and weeks go by post trip...we will enjoy sharing photos of the journey we took together and we'll do our best to remember the lessons we learned on the river.

MORE LESSONS LEARNED FROM THE RIVER...
LESSON LEARNED: "You get out of it what you put into it. It's all about your attitude."
LESSON LEARNED: "There are two types of fun; Type 1. Fun: when you're having a blast, and you know it and Type 2. Fun: like when you're into the middle of category 5 rapid and you're exhausted and concerned the boat's about to flip...but in reflection, it was epic fun!
LESSON LEARNED: You're a guest, in nature and on the boat...so be respectful. You are not entitled. "Don't tip-toe on the crypto"/"Don't hurt the dirt" / "Don't bust the crust"
LESSON LEARNED: "It doesn't matter what you look like, just that you're having fun".
LESSON LEARNED: I don't need a lot. I can reduce my life to a duffel bag and have everything I need"
LESSON LEARNED: "Being present can make the ordinary become extraordinary! Wherever you are – be ALL there! Notice; the light, the stars, the sound of conversation and laughter. Engage and REALLY talk.
LESSON LEARNED: "Do this – for as long as you can!
And finally... (all oars in the air)....One, Two, Three - RAPID FIRE!!!! (for life!)

Lisa and Tani Hansen-Burns

"We are artists my dear. We cannot be concerned with society's rules for us. We simply don't conform and why should we! We must take every moment, every ounce of beauty and live it. For then, we create with that moment in time something extraordinary to share with the world."

Kellie M Cox

A line from the novel, **Murderous Intent**. My favourite character, the extravagant Daniel is trying to persuade his author friend Samara to partake in yet another wickedly sinful activity.

THE ENERGY OF KINDNESS

Kindness was a common theme throughout the written pieces. What became apparent was not just the practice of kindness but the energy that is associated with kindness. I am not sure I had truly recognised before the energy that comes with the act of kindness. We have all heard the concept of paying it forward, one kind deed in turn creates another. There are often stories in our local community page about acts of kindness. One particular coffee shop drive through was in the media for the number of pay it forward acts in a row. It was something like ten customers who not only accepted the act of kindness but passed it forward or backward in this case to the driver of the car behind them in the drive through.

Kindness radiates like a light through a person's face. Think about it. Imagine the face of the person you think of when you think of kindness. It can be someone you know or a well know public figure. What does their face look like? What is their mouth doing as you picture them? What are their eyes saying? There is an undeniable look associated with people who embody kindness. It is not surprising that so many of my friends and family mentioned it in one way or another in their written pieces.

When I think of kindness, I imagine my workplace. Never before have I worked in a place where there are so many acts of kindness. I am only a contractor so pop into the office only on the days that I am required to complete an assessment. I have lost count of how many times there has been a random gift waiting for me. The other day it was a large Easter egg from the CEO. At other times, it is a freshly picked avocado from my manager's family farm. People bring in books to share, food to share, even a very special cutting of a rare red frangipani tree. And it is not only just gifts, but often a little note to someone to say congratulations, happy birthday, sharing a success of celebrations no matter how big or small.

There are walls of photos. Yes, photos are very big in my workplace. Happy snaps of group practical days, even happier snaps of recent graduates receiving their certificates. I have seen graduates who have completed their studies come in and spend hours assisting other students to complete their practicals by playing the client role for them when they have no one else to call on to assist.

Our group practical days are a real joy to experience, a group of six very nervous students come in to 'perform' the role of counsellor in a mock role play with other students playing the assigned client role. They have the pressure of not only having to complete an assessment which is either competent or not yet competent, but they also have to do so in front of a group of strangers. As the assessor, I jump in pretty quickly and get at least one assessment done before we have our first break. And that is all it takes. There are words of kindness, of compliments, of encouragement about what the student did well. They are making each other hot beverages; they are chatting away. These strangers within just a short period of time have become friends.

Most practical days, students finish the day exchanging numbers and laughing together as they leave the office. I am sure by now you can guess what course these students are studying. They are counsellors, youth workers and case managers. These students have decided to go into a profession that requires so much of them, not only professionally to learn the theories behind human development, but to become proficient in the skills and techniques required to support another person in their time of need.

There is much empathy required to perform these roles but also an underlying value of kindness. These roles require the professional to give so very much of themselves and above everything else to be kind to their clients and to themselves.

Kindness really is an energy and when experienced can become contagious. I am so honoured to be working with the people I work with. Staff and students who create this amazing energy that radiates not just from them but through them to others and ultimately, to people in community who need it more than anyone else - those that are finding themselves in the need of support from a kind professional.

There are so many pieces that fitted into this category but also fitted elsewhere. It is not surprising at all that the pieces included in this chapter are from counsellors and healers. Gorgeous people who are truly making a difference in the world.

Kellie M Cox

Spread kindness and love wherever you go. If you see someone who looks nice today, tell them, smile when you walk past strangers, ask how the cashier's day is and really listen, if you get great service from someone tell them and their manager, hold the door open for someone. It is incredible how much a small gesture like that can change someone's day. You will see happiness and gratitude fill their eyes, their smile will light up the room and in return you will feel amazing. It then starts a ripple effect of kindness and love. The best days I ever have start with small acts of kindness or a compliment, either from someone else or myself giving that to a stranger. It's like you open Pandora's box to happiness and spread it throughout your day. People are drawn to this energy and it spreads to them like wildfire. Give it a try, you will be so thankful you did.

Rhani Pearson, Counsellor, age 35.

The Artist Life

We share scenes
Words
Looks
Embraces
Understanding
Writing
Poetry
Portraits
Love
Lust
And our souls

Kellie M Cox

Life should be simple. Not easy, but relatively simple. Don't complicate it and make it harder by overthinking. Get out of your head and in to the moment. Too many people spend too much time waiting for things to get better; always looking for more instead of appreciating what they have. There is a peace that comes with not constantly craving for more; with appreciating where you're at, even if it's not where you want to be. Every season serves its purpose. But you have to be present to appreciate it. Surround yourself with the right people and wholeheartedly embrace the present - the opportunity and freedom that is the present. For it's here where you have the power to make your life what you want it to be.

If you want happiness, start creating it. Don't spend your time thinking that you're not enough or worrying about what others think. Happiness starts with you. Not with your job, not with your relationships, not with money, but with you. Be kind to yourself and spread that kindness everywhere. Be the well-wisher and the celebrator of the happiness of others. Shining for others doesn't dim your light, it makes the world shine brighter. Take the time to appreciate the moments when you feel like you're shining your brightest. Keep it simple- Recognise where you are, what you're doing, who you're with… then recreate and repeat those moments. Grow them, keep adding them to your life, and spread that light. With your happiness, like anything, if you want it, work at it every day until it flows. Create your reality. Shine & share- there's enough for everyone!

Be present. Be grateful. Be kind.

Nadine Meyn, age 32.

If you always tell the truth…you don't have
to have a good memory.

Sherry Wright

Life as I Know It

Something that I have always held as a core value in my life is to attempt to think before I act, speak, or judge a situation or person. This is especially important to me in regard to my relationships with others, be that my partner, children, family, friends or colleagues. Now of course I don't always succeed and that's part of being me, but I don't let these mishaps stop me from pursuing the goal.

I have throughout my life endeavored to consciously cultivate a heart and mind that is focused on celebrating other people's achievements, having an inquisitiveness of others and their journey through this life and choosing to see others through the lens of grace and kindness. By doing this I have noticed, the less my own life is caught up in judgement, jealousy, bitterness and unforgiveness. The freedom this gives from these negative, unhelpful feelings and emotions, brings a fuller life, rich in joy, peace, contentment, and more fulfilling relationships.

I'm also a great believer in being kind to the person in the mirror. It's taken me 55 years to come to grips with this, but every day I make a conscious decision to look in the mirror and say, "looking good girl!!!". This simple act is quite powerful as it sets my mind up for the day to focus on all the things in life I am grateful for, including all my lumps and bumps!

This way of life is not always easy, and I don't always get it right, but it's one I've found worth pursuing.

Jennifer Kamst

1. We get what we put up with.
2. It's all in the mind. We create our own reality with our thoughts, beliefs and emotions.
3. Do your best and accept the outcome. We create suffering when we judge and resist what is.
4. It's not so much what happens to us in life, that causes us pain but rather the meaning we give it.
5. In the whole universe, there's only one you. Find out who that is and share her/him with the world. We need you.
6. Be kind.

Christine Hyde, Healer, age 66.

Make happiness the priority

PT

LIVING LIFE WITH PASSION

Passion, the word itself evokes a smile on my face. I started this chapter very selfishly with my own blog from my travels. The blog I wrote as I was on a fast train leaving France. There is something about the city of Paris that eludes passion. It is the way the city vibrates, the people, the history, the fashion, the food, the unbridled resolve to live every moment to its fullest.

Many people who travel describe their very expensive pastime as a passion. Like kindness there is something deliriously contagious and highly addictive about finding your passion and living it. There is one concept that my friends like to ask me about time and time again. Who doesn't love a good travel story? My friends often ask about the French custom of taking a lover. I am not the expert in this field, I will state that up front but I, myself was fascinated with how it worked and had many conversations with newly acquired friends about it.

I won't do the explanation of the concept justice here and all I can really suggest is that if you want to understand the concept better, take a trip to Paris and find out for yourself. One friend over a vin rouge in a quaint little bar opposite The Louvre described it best. He said that as a Parisian born local, he grew up with a passion for life. He loved his long-term partner with great passion. He equally had much affection and emotion for his lover. One did not discount nor replace the other. Passion, potentially like love is boundless. He had passion to share with both people and he grew up to understand that there was no reason, no law, no ethic so great as to dissuade him from living his life of passion with both his partner and his lover, separately of course. They each knew of the other, as is the custom in France generally speaking.

In some ways he explained, it adds to both relationships. He would never leave his long-term partner but having the time apart to spend weekends away with his lover, trips to the South of France, dinners, drinks, this all created in him a fulfilment and fascination with life that he was able to share with his partner when he returned. There is nothing dishonest about his dealings and all parties of course have to be in agreement for these relationships to work.

In a similar vein a female French local friend of mine would invite me over to have a pajama party when her husband was spending the night with his lover. We would get comfy on the couch with the cat, drink delightful French wine and chat while watching movies. To be honest, there was a lot more chatting than movies, but that's what happens when you get friends together. She loved her husband very much but equally loved having the apartment to herself to enjoy having friends over when he wasn't home.

This life lived with passion in Paris extended into food. Dinner would begin with a walk to the local fromagerie and then the local boucherie to purchase the recommended best cheeses and cuts of the day. Meals were long affairs that came out in courses, each tantalising taste enjoyed to the fullest before the next plate was brought to the table. Local distilleries flouted their brew of the month and locals flocked to try the latest offerings. I enjoyed the most amazing freshly cut fruit salad drenched in locally distilled floral gin. There really is nothing like living each meal, each moment with passion. And doing so as the French do might take some practice for us less accustomed to living life to the fullest. If anyone else is like me my trips to the supermarkets are a face paced grab and dash without most of the time even thinking about what new combinations of food might be worth trying.

So, when you hear that I have once again taken off to Paris and before you ask me why I would return again, just imagine those meals and those conversations I am having and wish me luck in embracing every aspect of the French style of truly living a life of passion.

Many of my friends spoke of living a life with passion, which brought a huge grin to my face. I know these people and admire how they are embracing everyday of their life. I trust you will enjoy and hope you find inspiration to grab each and every second we have on this planet and do something wonderful with it.

Kellie M Cox

Blog Post
Paris… the City of Love

Paris, Paris… what can I say about Paris… the city that leaves her scent on your skin, your lips and your fingertips. She agitates you with desire, her power over confusing the succession of your thoughts. If Rome was the city of beauty, Paris must be the city of passion.

As I rented a gorgeous little apartment in the second district, I told my landlord it was to continue to write my blogs on her terrace. She had inspired me with her generosity of spirit. She was a deeply creative soul and with the magical powers of the arts she wished for me a muse, a muse to help me to create my very own fictional story of love.

And they came. With powers so strong, she conjured up not one, but many beautiful, creative, inspiring muses… photographers, writers, musicians, composers, singers and art history aficionados.

With these heady mix of characters at play, I soon envisaged myself, the poor impoverished writer, calling Paris home for a while. I wanted to soak up every ounce of their creativity. I wanted to live in their world, see what they see, share their emotional turmoil of the city that breathes passion.

Hours and hours talking with a very talented photographer with a brilliant mind about art, science, physics, philosophy, psychology, religion, family and home. He allowed me into his world for a short time meeting his eclectic groups of friends, now his family.

I felt embraced into their home, welcomed into their world as the insane Aussie travelling through Europe. The muses continued, the singer/composer/musician who loves artwork and found inspiration for music in the galleries and museums of Paris.

A fellow writer, a soulmate of sorts writing in her head all day, walking the streets with a smile as she conjures up the next sexy storyline of her plot. Living with her characters day and night as if they were friends she had always known.

The art history aficionado working so closely with the priceless treasures that surround him, knowing every inch of them in a way that the rest of us could only dream. Inspired by their beauty, richness and history he exuberated passion from every pore. His profound words ignite every sense in the body.

These were my muses. Each with their own savoir faire, so used to living with such greatness, the French have their very own word for it. Their savoir faire… for each it was different… culture, nature, anticipating, whispering words, writing, feeling, learning, touching, inspiring, being born to love, kissing… and yes, the Parisians love their kissing and speak of it often. These were their talents, their passions. I am sure there were many more hidden treasures they were too proud to assign.

My muses grant me my own savior-faire… charm, writing, imagination, perception and beauty. I accept them graciously. And as I feel more and more a part of their world, I start to question the notion of home. We chat about it, what makes a home, what is home, is it a place or a feeling? For one, it was friends, for another it was the culture of their home city of Paris, the place they were born. For another it was their family home, maybe a distant memory but the home they grew up in nevertheless. I am reminded time and time again that I live in one of the most beautiful natural countries in the world, a country that many could only wish to know.

I begin to wonder if I could one day call this city of passion home. As I write this last sentence on a train in the South of France, saying goodbye to this beautiful country, for now a mass of glistening blue water opens up before me beckoning me to stay basking in her glory. She is urging me to return.

So, my advice, and I'm not one to normally give advice, but you really should experience Paris, the home of parties of consumption and debauchery. And I jest with the city a little as I say that, but we all do know there is always some small element of truth to every legend.

If you come to Paris, don't listen to those who might say that the Parisians are rude people, that they won't speak English to you even though they can. Sure, see the sights, The Eiffel Tower, the Arc de Triomphe, Notre Dame, Champs Elysees, Moulin Rouge, the Palais Garnier and especially, The Louvre.

But please also meet the locals, the native born, the expats, the passionate blend of creative individuals who choose to call Paris home. Find your own savoir faire... learn theirs! And for those of you who might need their very own muse, let me know. I might try and see if some of their magical wonderment can be shared amongst friends.

Rome, you certainly taught me to appreciate beauty and a little of my heart remains with you but Paris you have left me undeniably changed forever. The passion that you have generously shared with me will inspire me always. I leave with you my beautiful muses. Take good care of them until I see them again.

Kellie M Cox

Great sex starts hours before you hit the bedroom! If you want great sex that is all about connection rather than just the physical act, then make love all day!

Find loving things to do for your partner during the day and by the time you are ready to go to bed there will be such a feeling of connection and safety that the sex is guaranteed to be fantastic.

Deb, age 70.

Life, Love, Luck & Laxatives

Life is a gift that you can't remember starting and won't remember ending, however it's the bits in between, which require cherishing. Whether it's those crazy people we meet along the way, the amazing experiences encountered or moments of absolute joy or despair, they all make us who we are.

I'm 52, I've been reckless, fun, foolish, serious, proud, loving, hateful, strong and weak, and they're all part of being human.
My life has been mostly a dream, with the occasional moments resembling nightmares!
I didn't let them crush me; I became stronger because of them.
When my younger brother was murdered, I stood on the beach and screamed "fuck you" into a cyclone; ending up with sand in places I didn't think possible.

When my now wife walked down the aisle 20 years ago on our wedding day, I cried tears of pure joy, the same goes for when our 2 beautiful kids were born.
Life has its up and downs, loves' come, some stay, others will go, energy ebbs and flows, it's why you feel awesome one day and shit the next.

Luck comes to us all, sometimes more than others; I've known a couple of people who if they slipped over in a dog shit, they'd find a diamond ring in it, lucky bastards!

As for laxatives, if you're having a bad day and feel the world just won't give you the break you've been looking for, pop a couple, grab a book or the fully charged iPad, put up the "do not disturb" sign on the door and expel those demons.

I've learnt a lot but have so much more to experience, one thing I do know is that the treadmill of life keeps spinning, don't get stuck on it, look forwards, not backwards as your past has got you to the present, the future is where your life is at, make it a good one!

BJ, age 52.

Watch "Yes Man" with Jim Carrey - not because it's a particularly good movie, but because the message "Say yes to whatever comes your way" reflects the whole point of being alive.

Don't live a small life - make it BIG and ever–expanding. Every day brings the experience of uncertainty, and that can be uncomfortable. But if you say "Yes" to the uncertainty and do it anyway, the discomfort of "not knowing" lessens and your power rebuilds.

Nothing better than looking back in the second half of life and knowing you've been maxing your opportunities!

Phil, Boundary Spanner, age 61.

Advice for Life...

Nothing ever is the same, including opinions and beliefs we KNOW (we think we know) to be "true" and live / act by.
Life will CHANGE these perspectives- so live your own life with a pinch of salt.
And at the same time commit.
At the same time, if you are going to do something, do it with (to quote a friend of mine) 'head heart and hands". That is bring your heart and head to what you are doing.

Live to serve others/ the whole.

Be courageous to communicate what needs to be said.

BE bold and go outside the box, take what feels like risks, but is really just being awesome.

Make the effort.

No regrets. No mistakes. Only adventures.

SING!

Keep building your connection with Mother Earth and community.

Listen.

"No expectations, full participation"

Know how to close your eyes and go within, close off the outside world for a sec.

Liz Lecoanet

Love life to the max
Spread love to those around you
And overall have fun

Georgia

A Life Lived with Passion

My passion for storytelling has been with me since I was two years old. I would sit at the table and draw stick figure characters in comic-strip like sequences, and my mum would sit with me and listen to me telling her my stick figure stories. My dad kept me supplied with reams of recycled paper to draw on from his office workplace. My drawing 'stories' continued to evolve and improve over the years until finally I stopped drawing my stories and started writing them.

From a very young age I knew that I wanted to be an author, and I even remember my dad conducting an 'interview' with me in which I declared this. It felt strange to be so sure of my life passion and purpose so young, and while my peers were searching for theirs, I thought that maybe I was missing something, or choosing the wrong path. My goals and aspirations were perceived as unconventional by some, and I have had plenty of doubts about the legitimacy of my passion over the years. I always believed I was good enough to be a 'success'- I defined success back then as getting published- but I was concerned that the pursuit of my passion was not practical enough for 'real' life. It wasn't until I removed the need for my life purpose to be profitable that I was fully able to embrace it and commit to it.

My writing has seen me through many of life's challenges. I struggled to learn the traditional way in the classroom, and like so many experienced bullying. When I would struggle at school, I would come home in the afternoon and write my stories. It was an escape, something that I was good at when other tasks were difficult. My tertiary education has been mostly informal; while my peers were headed off to university, I completed a correspondence writing course and attended as many local writing workshops that I could afford. I saw many friends drop in and out of university courses on their search for connection to something of interest to them, and I couldn't see the point in this; I knew that I wanted to write and be a published author, and so I felt that my time was best spent pursuing this. I knew what I wanted to do with my life, and at the time it did not involve traditional study. I did not see the point in accumulating debt for education that I was not completely invested in, and it was not until I was thirty that I finally identified a study path I was truly passionate about. Besides writing, I am also a trained circus performer specialising in hula hooping. I saw an opportunity to incorporate my circus skills into fitness activities and am currently studying to become a personal trainer specialising in circus skills.

Writing is part of who I am. I love the sheer passion I feel when I write. I love the daily sense of achievement – reaching small goals and then eventually fulfilling the big goals while enjoying what I am doing along the way. I cannot imagine life without my passion, and what day-to-day life would be like if writing wasn't a part of it. I feel incredibly fortunate that, with the exception of a few, I have had family that have always encouraged and guided me to pursue my writing passion.

My life purpose has always been very clear to me, and I realise how special this is. Most people spend years wondering and searching for what sets their soul on fire. I do believe that everyone already knows what that something is at some level, whether they are aware of it or not, but even when they have some idea, it is often met with such resistance by the human mind. We have to work hard to move through the limitations of our own thoughts and beliefs to allow ourselves to realise and engage with our life's passion.

As with everything that happened during our upbringing, when we become adults, we must stop looking back at the shortcomings of our parents and take responsibility for our own lives, in the pursuit of discovering and nurturing our passions. While for the most part I was supported by my family, there were those who disapproved when I first started taking my writing seriously as a teenager and young adult. At that time, I felt very resentful towards those individuals for their lack of support, but now I realise that they were simply speaking from the perspective of their own experiences and belief systems. In fact, by actively engaging with and visibly pursuing my writing and publishing goals, I experienced the perspectives of these individuals shift, and as a result they realised the importance of having passion in life.

While support is beneficial and invaluable, it is not the responsibility of anyone else to motivate us to discover our life's purpose and passion. That is something we need to do for ourselves on an individual basis, by taking radical responsibility for discovering our life's passions. This process will require some self-enquiry, to dig deep and ask what it is that you are drawn to. When support and encouragement doesn't come from family, colleagues or existing social circle, this is when you need to go out and find that support system for yourself. There are many community groups and business organisations, in person and online, that support and nurture various hobbies and vocations. There is a group and community for just about anything these days!

We humans are creative beings, and creativity is not restricted to the arts. For example, cooking is a very creative activity. I know professional people who have an amazing talent for cake decorating! I struggled for a long time to believe in my life's passion for writing because although I loved it, I did not believe it was a legitimate life path to choose, and I didn't feel like a contributing member of society. It wasn't until I was almost thirty that I realised that my life's passion did not have to be mainstream or profitable, and it was quite acceptable for it to not make me much, if any, money. This realisation was a game changer for me, something that really helped me take ownership of and commit to my passion. I allowed myself to fully step into my life's purpose, and I could finally let myself be who I was always meant to be. I have a job and meet my financial responsibilities, but my main focus is outside of my workplace.

In our society we are so focused on success and can tend not to try something new if we don't think we'll be that good at it, or if we won't make money from it. For a long time, I felt I had to legitimise my passions for writing and performing by trying to make a career of these things, and around 2015-16 I felt I had to choose between my writing and circus performing and focus on one in order to give it the attention it needed around my other work commitments. I chose writing- my part-time job meant I was taking less and less circus performance opportunities, and there were a few years when I didn't do any hula hooping at all. In 2019, I started hula hooping again, this time just for my own fitness and enjoyment. It was quite confronting to do this, when there was no real end result attached, for example a performance I was preparing for. To do this activity just for the pure enjoyment of it was a very foreign concept. I felt the same about my writing; since I first began taking my writing seriously at age eighteen, publishing was my main motivation, and in the ten years that followed I spent more time learning about and engaging in book marketing and promotion that actual writing. In 2020 when the COVID-19 pandemic hit, I put my publishing goals to the side for the most part and returned to the simple act of writing. Everyone was so distracted by the world events we were facing, and emotionally and mentally drained, so I figured it was a waste of time trying to convince them to buy my books. I discovered during this time that at its core my writing was for me, and I have learned how to return to the pure joy of writing. I have remembered how to write just for me. To distract me, to lift my spirits. And if you too are struggling, I encourage you to seek out what you love, and do more of that. While your passion may serve others in the form of providing a product or service, ultimately it is something you do for yourself. Not for your kids, or your partner, or your family. While it may benefit them, in the form of extra income or simply setting a positive example, your passion starts with you, and you need to do it for you.

My creativity is so important to me, and vital it is to my mental health and emotional well-being. While I still set goals and have a vision for publishing, I have detached from my old ideals of success, and reconnect even more with the simple act of writing. No matter how my publishing goals change and shift, one thing has stayed consistent for me and that is the act of writing itself. As always, writing has served as a source of strength and inspiration to me. A way to lift my spirits, a place to escape when the real world becomes too much. I have had to let go of so much in regard to my publishing experience and what I thought that would look like, but my writing experience remains untouched. The same goes for my circus performing. These days I practice hula hooping tricks to further my own skill, to explore what my body is capable of, to challenge myself and to push my own limits. As a result, I develop my skill anyway, and my audiences enjoy my performance. My performances are usually themed, and this is just another channel that I express myself as a storyteller. No matter what happens in the external world, I will always have the simple, joyful act of storytelling.

Kate Kelsen, Author, age 31.

Advice For A Long Life

Keep healthy, eat lots and exercise lots.
Keep in touch with your friends, the real friends.
Sleep deep, but don't hibernate.
Awake and attack the day
But not the people around you.
Don't be so serious on the computer,
Smile, and relax your shoulders,
and have a good belly laugh now and then.
Dream and keep on dreaming,
The horizon is really close.
Enjoy a hobby that you can take into retirement,
Drink cocktails and wine and beer,
and cocktails and wine and beer.
Variety is entertainment,
So, what is the spice of life,
and what, is 'moderation'?

David Kay, Author, www.davidthomaskay.com

LIFELONG LEARNING

I am in a number of writing groups, and you always get that one person who doesn't want to do the workshop, they don't want to hear the guest speaker, because they know it all already. One of my author friends, upon seeing this, reflected on a quote she had heard.

If you are the smartest person in the room, you are likely to be in the wrong room.

I don't know who to attribute those words to. One of the contributors shared a similar thought. They said that the older they get, the more they realised they don't know. This speaks much to the wisdom of years. One of the reasons for bringing this book to life was to share my friends' wisdom and lessons learnt from life. I jokingly referred to being wise at fifty. But maybe the wisdom begins at that point that you realise you will never be the smartest person in the room.

Much of my learnings lately have come from the cohorts that would be identified under the labels Gen Z and Gen Y. I am apparently labelled a Gen X, although only the other day, someone referred to themself and I as Baby Boomers, which would make me at the very least 57 years old. I didn't correct them. I must have looked a bit rough that day.

Many of my recent clients have fallen into this age range, as do my adult children. There is something to their values around work/life balance. Some people have called the Gen Z and Ys entitled and lazy, but when you actually hear what is behind their life choices, it really does make sense. They have shared their dislike of full-time work, of thinking it isn't the right balance for a healthy and enjoyable life. And most people I know would agree. Many of us 'older' people, and I use that term sparingly, were raised in a society that told us to do well at school, go to university, find a career and work in it five days out of seven days every week, until we retire and can finally enjoy our life. There are so many elements wrong with the old school mentality, firstly and most importantly, many of us do not even live to reach retirement and those that do, find the limited savings are barely conducive to the carefree nomadic lifestyle we might have been sold.

Not only do we not live long enough to retire but many are health compromised because of holding down stressful full-time positions for decades on end. And that is of course for those fortunate enough to be able to be gainfully employed until retirement. If recent times have shown us nothing more, it is that nothing is permanent. Many a commercial pilot living the dream life of a career in the skies, seeing the world, cushioned by large salaries are now mowing lawns and nothing wrong with moving lawns but it wasn't what many of them imagined doing in the year 2020.

So, if we can take the time to look beyond our position and status in life and embrace the rewards of being a lifelong learner, we will have much to learn from the generations before and after.

My clients teach me so much. Not just about my clinical practice, but also about human behaviour, strength and resilience. There isn't a session in which I not only further develop my clinical skills but also learn something new, even if it is the smallest of things. I will never be the smartest person in the room and how grateful I am that is the case. How boring would life be if we reached a certain point, where we knew everything already.

Many of my friends wrote about lessons learnt. This chapter could have been so much longer. Hope you the reader, enjoy their stories as much as I did.

Kellie M Cox

Not Advice... Just Some Learnings

They say that our youngest years (aged 3-5) are the most critical for brain development. These years help shape our social and emotional abilities and learning skills. This may be true, but I have to say that *every* decade of my life has brought with it development and learning which influences who I am, what I see (and don't see) and how I am able to emotionally regulate myself through times of stress!

I am the last person on earth to give anyone advice on how to live their life. Truth be told, I'm 'winging it' myself! So instead of advice, here is a collection of some of the quirky, mundane, scary and inspiring learnings that have helped shape my life so far as I also near that half century milestone.

Frog on a Log

Since an early age I have had a very vivid imagination. One morning, four-year-old Melissa woke a little later than usual and spied Mum walking from the clothesline with a washing basket tucked under her arm.

We lived on a steep bushland block, not far from the city of Sydney, and the clothesline was located next the creek which ran down the back boundary of our yard. This area provided myself and my brothers with hours of entertainment as we caught tadpoles with a tea-strainer, swung on the gathered leaves of the weeping willow tree, and jumped over the rocks in search for lizards and crickets.

My mother told me that I had just missed out on the most amazing sight as she had witnessed a whole family of frogs, perched on a log across the creek, croaking in chorus.

Now, I don't know whether she was actually telling me the truth or not, but just the *idea* of seeing a whole family of singing frogs really stirred my imagination.

From that day forward, every morning I would wake early and earnestly look out the window to see if I could catch a glimpse of the 'von Trapp Family' of frogs.

What did I learn? Seize the day! Get up early, because *that* is when all the magic happens.

Pig-tales

Wearing pigtails adorned with blue satin ribbons, Melissa in first grade was a real 'goodie goodie'.

The teacher's seating plan had placed me next to Gregory, who, on reflection, was a bit of a rascal. He had ginger hair, freckles and a smile that always indicated that he was up to something.

One day, I was just minding my business, working in earnest as I carefully traced the Cursive letters on the violet-coloured mimeograph handout placed in front of me, when I was above to get a rude surprise.

Gregory had spied a purple-coloured bruise above my knee and it was just *too* tempting. He aggressively pushed his bony little finger deeply into it!

I yelped out in pain and my body automatically leapt out of the seat.

The teacher was not at all pleased with my behaviour, disciplined me for disturbing the class and was not the least bit interested in my reasons for doing so. I was absolutely mortified, as this was the first time I had ever been in trouble.

So, what did I learn: There are always going to be people in the world who will gain great pleasure from pressing your bruises. Don't give them the added pleasure of a reaction which reflects badly on yourself.

Blow-Out

It felt like slow motion as the car swerved across the highway, became air bound and then rolled three times down the embankment. My whole family, my world, were in that car. I was 13 years of age and we were on a road trip to the Great Barrier Reef.

Whilst we rolled, over, and over, and over again, I thought, "I am thinking, therefore, I am still alive… but what about my family? Will they survive? Will I be left alone on this earth?"

Finally – stillness. After a brief second that felt like an eternity, we all started calling out to each other – "Are you ok? Answer me!"

We had to get out, fast. Fuel was leaking from the tank and it would only take one spark and the car could ignite.

The car was upside down. Contorting my body to reach across my two younger brothers, together, we kicked the back side window out and crawled out. I led them to safety, away from the car and then looked back. Our parents were still trapped in the crumpled mess and we could hear them calling out to us. I had a decision to make at that moment. Did I stay with my brothers and wait for help (if it came on this lonely country stretch of highway)? Or, did I risk going back to the wreck, to help my parents to escape?

If I stayed with my younger brothers and the car became engulfed in flames, I could still care for them, but we would all be without parents. If I went to help my parents and the car blew up, myself and my parents would all be gone, and my younger brothers would be alone. The decision to go back and help my parents get out of the car was one of the most difficult decisions of my life.

My mother had managed to climb over the seats to get to the back window, so I helped pull her out of the twisted metal. Dad was next – but he was a lot bigger and needed to crawl through the small gap between the front seats to access the window at the back. I was aware of time; the petrol was still pouring out of the tank. Dad couldn't fit though the back window as his shoulders were too wide. The only way he could get out was via the back door, however the car was leaning into the earth and so the door couldn't be opened. The side of the car needed to be lifted in order to prise the door open.

When faced with an emergency, our brains and bodies are designed to get us out of danger. I was able to think very clearly, and my body was able to perform (what would normally be considered) an impossible feat. At 13 years of age, I lifted the weight of a Mitsubishi Sigma sedan to help get my dad out of the car wreck.

Love is what drove me. And adrenalin!

We all survived, a little battered and bruised – but it really is a miracle that we are all here to tell the story. The car was a write-off. After a visit to the local hospital at Gin Gin, we went back to a motel and expected that our dream holiday to the Great Barrier Reef was over. However, the next morning, Mum and Dad surprised us all by vowing to continue on the trip. Dad caught a lift into the next major town, hired a car, and we had one of the best holidays of our lives.

Learnings (there are more than one for this life experience!): 1. Life is so precious and can change in a split second. 2. You have more strength than you realise. 3. Never give up – don't let the obstacles stop you from living a life of joy. 4. Your greatest learnings come from your greatest challenges.

Friends are the Family You Choose

When you find a friend who truly 'gets you', a weight is lifted off your shoulders. You can laugh together until your bellies hurt, you can cry, you can grow. I will be forever grateful for finding my lifelong friend, Kellie Cox when we were 15 years of age.

From the moment we met, we knew that we were two peas in a pod. We could finish each other sentences and explode into laughter over incidents that required no explanation. We got up to mischief together, as teenage girls often do. We formulated plans and goals for our future based on all the extensive wisdom that we had at that time :-). Somehow, we managed to come through our teenage years relatively unscathed. I think a big part of that comes down to always having each other's back. Through the moves, boyfriends, divorces, career changes, children and ups and downs of life - we always kept in touch and inspired each other to be the best we could be. I can honestly say that there has never been any 'judgement' between Kellie and I, only love and encouragement. That type of friendship is GOLD.

Learning: *True* friends are rarer than most people realise. They bring out the best in you, encourage you and love you for who you are. Plenty of people will come and go through your life, but there will be a select number of very special people who stay in your heart, mind and life. These people are precious. They know your soul. Treasure them.

Kellie Cox, my darling friend. I love you and am so grateful to travel this winding journey of life with you.

Perception is Reality

Three weeks into a three-month overland safari in Africa – I was living the dream. I was about to visit the mountain gorillas in their natural habitat between the countries of Zaire (now known as the Democratic Republic of Congo) and Rwanda. Within years of visiting this area, millions of lives would be lost in uprisings and wars; however, at 21 years of age, I was quite oblivious to any dangers.

One of my biggest learnings in life was obtained as I sat outside my tent observing local village life. Despite the poverty and the danger present, I witnessed an African woman sweeping out the dirt floor of her hut, singing and smiling. She found joy in that moment – I could see it in her face.

What did I learn from witnessing this?

Happiness is an internal experience and very much shaped by perception, gratitude and an appreciation of the moment.

The woman I observed lived with more challenges than I will likely ever experience and yet, she managed to feel joy and peace in that moment.

We don't have control over our circumstances in life, but we *do* have control over how we perceive them, and therefore our internal experience of life. This beautiful woman on the other side of the world, taught me this and I am forever grateful.

Walk in My Shoes

The lines between virtue and vice can be blurred.

I had made a commitment, marriage, involving vows exchanged in the presence of God, family and friends. But four years on, the relationship wasn't what I thought it would be. My dreams and hopes of having a happy partnership and family were being crushed.

I spoke to my local priest, a very wise and kind man. His advice to me was, "Melissa, you are young, you still have the opportunity to have family and happiness. If your husband is not willing to change - then God does not expect you to be a martyr." Whoa! That was my lifeline.

I left that abusive relationship. In a different culture, religion, place, or decade, leaving a marriage could be considered 'sinful'.

What did I learn? The lines between virtue and vice can be blurred. There are no definite 'rights' and 'wrongs' in life – so reserve judgement and just follow love.

Birth is Sacred

Giving birth can and should be, one of the most beautiful and transformational times in a mother's life. I knew this intuitively, but society was presenting a different story. Every depiction of birth in the media (and stories shared by other women) seemed to involve trauma and the highest level of pain any person could ever endure.

I had met my soulmate, Stephen. We had married and were now expecting our first baby. I wanted to ensure that I gave our baby the best start in life and have a natural birth if possible, however, there was a catch – I was REALLY scared about the pain of giving birth!

Having said that, it still didn't make logical sense to me that the beginning of life could be surrounded by so much pain and trauma. So, I went searching for answers. Firstly, I researched the relationship between fear and traumatic births. I could definitely see a correlation and evidence backs this up! So, I learnt how to use self-hypnosis, deep relaxation and utilised breathing and other techniques to remove fear, reduce tension and stay calm and positive through pregnancy, labour and birth. I also built my knowledge about birth so I could make informed decisions and ensured that I had great support.

Only minutes after birthing our first baby, I turned to my husband and said, "Let's do this again!". I was on such a high and felt like I had just climbed Everest! I had complete clarity and was primed to start my parenting journey in the most positive way.

I went on to use and perfect this approach to birth for my 2nd and 3rd babies. All of my births were beautiful calm and connected. I felt completely empowered after each birth. I want ALL parents to experience this. It is our birth-right!

My approach to birth has actually changed my life – professionally and personally. I incorporated a combination of tools, techniques, knowledge and support into a method of preparation for a positive and empowered birth. I have since written parent courses for natural, assisted and caesarean births (Hypnobirthing Australia™ and Hypnobubs™ programs) and they have become Australia's most popular childbirth education courses taught independently, online and through major health services. I have also co-written BirthCourse™ which is being used for research and taught in several major hospitals in Australia.

What I learned: When you find something that you are passionate about and make it your life mission, you can make a very positive impact on your own life and the world. Follow your dreams with determination, persistence and joy. But remember… passion is wasted without *action*.

The Older I Get, the Less I Know

Back in my 20s I studied some philosophy at university. I had always been intrigued by the teachings of Socrates, but it took me until 49 years of age to finally get what he meant by, "The only true wisdom is in knowing you know nothing."

What I am learning now: It is a strange peculiarity about life... the older I am, the less I know! There are so many blurred lines. Often those who speak the loudest and with the most conviction are the ones people listen to – but this doesn't mean they are speaking the truth. As the years go on, I realise how often my own and other's perceptions and beliefs can be incorrect. Considering the complexity of this universe, we *all* know nothing. Humans can (and often are) incorrect in our 'facts' and 'understandings' of how the body, world and life work. I guess I had to age a bit in order to come to this realisation. Luckily, my children are now reaching their teenage years and so they guide me from this point forward, as they know everything! Lol.

Melissa Spilsted

What I needed to hear!

Sometime around my 50th Birthday, I had an epiphany. I realised that until that point, I'd been living my life on other peoples' terms, eager to please, afraid of appearing foolish, fostering the classic imposter syndrome. After contemplating this revelation for some time, I began to trace it back to my early childhood.

I grew up in the 1960s and 70s in a Midlands suburb which, at that time, was voted the most violent place in England. Sounds horrific, but to us kids, life there was perfectly normal because we didn't know any different. I was what you would call a late bloomer. I remember being the last kid in class to learn to read, I struggled with spelling and maths, and pretty much every other subject. I left school at 15. Teachers wouldn't be allowed to say such a thing nowadays, but I was told I'd never amount to anything, and it was suggested I join the army…if they'd have me.

My first job was at a local factory where a mate worked. I hated it but ended up staying there for ten years. At 16 I had no idea of which way my life was going. It was 1980, alcohol, music, fashion, and of course, girls were the only things on my mind at that time. The biggest and by far the greatest thing that happened to me was when I met my future wife, Jane. We were 17.

We've been together for 41 years and married for 38 years. We settled into a normal working-class life, mortgage, two kids and a dog. We were happy, but as the years passed, we began to realise that if we stayed the same, there would be very little prospect of progressing much further in life.

So, we decided to make a change. In 1989, we emigrated to Australia. Sight unseen, we sold the house, packed up the belongings and got on a plane to Brisbane. Compared to our lives in the UK, life in Queensland was heavenly. Although family life will always have its ups and downs, for the first time we actually found ourselves looking forward to the future, rather than dreading it as we did in the UK.

So, what happened when I reached 50?

I never seem to take into consideration the 99% of positive things that have happened in my life, the achievements, the accolades, the complements. After realising that it was the 1% of negatives that had been driving me, I purposely started to focus on the positives, of which there are many.

At this time of writing, I run my own publishing company, I'm The President of the Gold Coast Writers Association, and author of 9 books. I live at the beach on the Gold Coast, I have two beautiful granddaughters, and have travelled the world.

I often reflect on my childhood. That kid with no future. And I wonder if his life would have turned out differently if I'd been able to travel back in time and offer him my advice. Well, to find out, that's exactly what I did. Through my meditation practice I watch him on the street where he grew up. He's about 8 years old. The other parents don't like their kids playing with him because he's a cheeky little bugger, always getting in trouble. I've observed the interaction with his friends, the little chameleon willing to do anything to fit in. On this occasion I see him coming towards me, alone with a football under one arm. He's in a hurry, late for dinner no doubt, but it's time to make contact.

'Hey kid,' I call out.

He squints at me warily through National Health glasses. He's scruffy. The jumper that his grandma knitted has stretched to about two sizes too big. His shorts are ripped and the plimsolls on his feet are dirty and torn. But for some reason, I don't feel pity. This takes me by surprise. Instead, I find myself feeling proud of him. I realise that although this kid has got a long hard struggle in front of him, he makes it regardless.

'Don't ever worry about what anyone else says or thinks.' The line I'd rehearsed suddenly sounds pathetic. He frowns.

'People are going to be mean and nasty to you,' I continue. 'But don't let them upset you, and more importantly don't let them change you.'

'Who are you?' he finally asks.

At first, I don't answer. I just look at him and begin to wonder if I'm doing the right thing. I'm trying to remember the thought process at that age and realise I can't.

'Just be you, kid.' I place a hand on his shoulder. 'Believe in yourself. You are the greatest!'

His confused expression tells me that he's never heard this before, and he blushes. But after a moment's thought, he squints at me again. 'Can I give you some advice?'

'Sure,' I say, taken aback.

'Don't dwell on the past. Concentrate on the present and the future will take care of itself!'

Wow! I wasn't expecting this. The kid I'd felt sorry for all my life is actually giving me advice? 'Thanks!' is the only response I can find.

He shrugs. 'You're welcome.'

I watch him as he skips away without a care in the world and realise he's a lot smarter and tougher than I remember. But of course, he had to be to survive. Beneath my breath, I thank him again for his advice. I close my eyes and reflect on this for a while. My aim had been to go back and give my younger self the advice I thought he needed to hear. When in fact he ended up giving me the advice I needed to hear. Cheeky little bugger!

Andy McDermott

Harsh but Critical Advice

While a student at the National Institute of Dramatic Art in the early 1990's, I participated in a performance workshop conducted by a visiting Russian acting pedagogue. After one particular exercise, I received a piece of acting advice from this man I'll never forget. His words exactly were, "It was good, but it was shit."

Now on face value, this type of critique may seem harsh to some, particularly by 2021 standards. Still, I was able to comprehend what lies beneath the line and its salient message. That being, even when you think you've done the best you can, you can always do better.

Close enough is never good enough. Always keep striving to better yourself every day. I have attempted to continue to live by those words my Russian friend once offered to me, particularly when it comes to acting. Why? Because I want tomorrow's performance to exceed the one I gave today, and, ultimately, I want to be a better person tomorrow than I was today.

Stu Lumsden, Actor, Teacher, age 49.

The Power Within

As a tiny child, I was powerful.

I received all the love, affection, support and encouragement anyone could ever dream of. My parents were loving and cheered on my charming quirkiness! They applauded my vivacious and creative nature and they encouraged me to be whatever I wanted to be!
They enabled me to express myself freely and grow into a vibrant and emotionally stable young child. Without even being aware of it…I was powerful.

As I grew, I was forever confident knowing that I could be and do anything I set my mind to. Deep within my soul, I felt an all-embracing comfort, knowing that I would succeed in life, no matter what. I would live a life that I chose and that I truly deserved.
They taught me well. They taught me self-love and to always be proud of ME.

Unfortunately, we don't always heed the lessons we are taught or shown as children. Along the path, we often lose that self-assuredness and quiet confidence we held within. As we grow, we are more susceptible to outside influence; the stresses and pressures of our peers, our teachers, our lovers. We often quite unknowingly, enable those around us, to weaken our power and break down our "childlike" confidence. We allow their negativity to seep into our souls and diminish our internal light.

Recently, during a candid conversation with my 87-year-old mother, she told me that, she was filled with joy to finally see "her Marisa" return. The Marisa who at 21 could have ruled the world. Could have chosen any path and succeeded. The Marisa who was forever smiling, sparkling like a diamond from within. She was teary eyed as she told me this and I believed her. I knew exactly what she meant.

At the young age of 21, I met the man who I truly believed to be the love of my life. I was young, effervescent, starry-eyed and eager to live a life of excitement and adventure with him. I have no regrets as such. I lived an incredible life in the eyes of many, including my own, however the power he exercised over me, was the catalyst to me losing much of my self esteem and power.

Over a period of many years, I enabled behaviour that slowly but surely eroded my very essence.
I lost my self confidence.
I felt unworthy of greatness or success.
I was made to feel useless and incapable of achieving anything of value.
I endured mental abuse that wore down my sense of self worth and left me scarred.
I felt empty and had lost my beautiful sparkle that my mother often spoke of.
In fact, although I smiled and outwardly portrayed the happy wife, there was an overwhelming sadness in my eyes. A sadness that stemmed from deep within my soul and was impossible to hide.

It is only now, with age and much gathered wisdom, that I realise I enabled others to 'chip away' at my power. To dull the light that once shone so brightly and to peel away the layers of self love that I had built up when younger.

It took many years to rebuild my power and regain my inner strength. To truly find Marisa and allow her to shine once more.

At almost 60, I continue to learn and have so many lessons I could share with you today but having to choose just one, my advice would be this.

Never lose your power of self.
Never enable others to make you feel small or insignificant.
Never allow that beautiful, blinding light that shines so brightly from your soul to be tainted or extinguished because of something or someone.

You have the innate power to achieve anything you believe in.
You have the inner force and strength to move mountains!
You have the capability to succeed in whatever to choose to pursue.

You are truly beautiful inside and out.
You are unique in every way.
You have the right to enjoy abundance in your life.
You are a miracle.

Believe in yourself because you hold the power within.

Marisa Raoul

Email: raoulmarisa@gmail.com
Website: www.marisaraoul.com
Instagram: www.instagram.com/marisaraoul

To the master of many things, voyager and eternal student. I will share some advice from my existence on Earth.

Many people will offer different forms of advice that resonates with them, you must find what connects with you and carry it into your daily routine.

And look back for things you have forgotten and passed over might have a stronger impact in 5,10,20 years.

1. Find out what your programming has been, we are all programmed since birth, what to; think, like, respect, avoid, do, etc. Once you open your mind to the way you think, then you can start to master yourself and adjust to be more pleased with your choices rather than your programming's choice.

2. Love yourself, learn to let go of external barriers that have stopped you thus far. You are not your body. Respect the vehicle that allows you this journey of life.

3. Learn to let go of circumstances; surrounding your life, job, education, reasons why or why not. Then accept them and move towards your goal whatever it may be. This takes time.

4. Compound interest. Einstein wasn't wrong when he said it's one of man's greatest creations. Make sure that you learn how to use it to your advantage and not be taken advantage of it. The earlier the better.

5. Follow your heart (gut, intuition). Know when to use your brain and know when your gut is right. Life is a journey, and the heart allows you adventures.

6. Learn to be happy by yourself without anyone or anything. You don't always have to be busy or filling your mind with stuff. You'll never be lonely if you master this.

7. Know when to let your love go. If you and your partner have different journeys to take, that's OK. It's hard to do this one but this physical world allows for many different connections. And not every relationship is forever, we are on this train and we get off at different stops. Look at your parents. Birth also means death.

8. Enjoy the moment. It's OK not to take a picture or video when you are somewhere, and things are happening.

9. Even the strongest become lost, weak, lonely, tired or want to give up. Breathe, calm your mind, rest and allow yourself time to heal.

Even when all feels lost. You will become strong again if you let yourself.

10. Appreciate peoples' time. Life is short. A conversation with your Mum, Dad, friend or someone close will have meaning to you. And even more meaning when that person is gone and not in your life. when you are with people you care about, listen absorb and live in the moment.

11. Forgive. There is no point hurting yourself because of something that has happened. No matter what it is, holding; hurt, pain or anger toward someone hurts you and the other person normally gets on with their life.

12. Listen. when people are talking to you, put your phone down, look at them and listen. It's a shame our society uses hears things, but listening is understanding. And to do that takes energy.

13. Smile. It's tremendous. It's also contagious. :)

Dean Mayer, Actor, Voice-Over, Director, Producer.

COURAGE BEYOND WORDS

This chapter is inspiring. The strength and resilience of my friends is truly incredible. And resilience is the word that kept popping into my head as I read all the stories my friends shared with me. Resilience isn't possible without courage. The two go hand in hand.

One of my greatest learning experiences came when I read the book *The Survivor Personality* about twenty years ago. I was working with children and young people, many of whom came from complex trauma backgrounds. I read the book and it resonated with me so much, that I emailed the author. On a side note, this is something I have done more than once, and it is wonderful when you actually hear back from the author. Try it sometime!

The author, a renowned psychologist and ex-paratrooper emailed me back. He was keen to hear what I took from the book into my work with children. This email exchange began a mentorship that spanned several years. Communication was long and complex with this particular psychologist as for each and every time I asked a question, I received a question in return. I just wanted to soak up every wisdom this clinician had to share but he lived his life as he theorised by believing that resilience cannot be taught but can be learnt.

Over the course of our communications, I learnt about

resilience. Not just that out of a bad situation, a person can bounce back, but of true resilience. Which is that out of a bad experience or situation, a truly resilient person will become better than they were before – stronger, smarter, more aware, more capable. I had always hoped to study in Portland with the author but unfortunately, it wasn't meant to be.

After his passing, I went to his website to share my condolences with his family only to read many other stories like mine. People who for personal or professional reasons had reached out and sought advice from the respected psychologist. People from all around the globe, shared their stories of learning and growth and how their own resilience was shaped by their informal mentorship with this wise man.

It takes courage to be strong, not the other way around. You don't have to be strong to be courageous, but you do have to have the belief and determination to be a better person with each new day. I hope you enjoy the courage each of the following writers have to share.

Kellie M Cox

If It Has Got To Be… Then It Is Up To Me!

These are words I have lived by since I was 28yo and met my first mentor, a lady called Ms Patt Smith.

Patt was a terrific 'people person' and encouraged not only myself, but many others; to follow their dreams. She advised that if I really wanted to do something or get anywhere in life, then I had to define what I wanted, do some research and make a plan then get on with getting things done.

I have applied Patt's wisdom to many parts of my life. She encouraged me to go on and complete some formal study. A path denied to me by my parents, especially my father who believed that education was for the males in the family. My father stated many times that girls just married and have children and don't need an education. He had a very old school approach, but I guess with six (6) children and a small business to run, my father couldn't afford to keep his girls in education.

Patt valued the empowerment of women, especially education. She believed that knowledge provided competence, and through competence a person gained confidence. Patt mentored me through my first tertiary course and attended my first graduation ceremony. My parents were invited but declined to attend. I went on after that to complete many other tertiary courses which led me down a varied employment journey to senior management level and held positions on a variety of Boards, even president of state-wide industry association.

But Patt's words came to me in dark times too. In 1996 my marriage was under strain. My husband was a fly-in/fly-out worker and often away for months at a time. This put a lot of pressure on me to run the family home, get three (3) children to school and afterschool sports and other activities, plus hold down paid employment.

During one of his many trips away to Papua New Guinea, I had a visit from my parents. They now lived interstate as my family had to move twice for my husband's employment. At that time, I had a model of a car called a 'Blue Bird', actually the car was white in colour. My parents said that the car's name was spot on as I would 'fly-in and fly-out' picking up and dropping off children.

I would rush home from work, no doubt speeding at times. I would pick up two (2) children from school, a quick trip home to get something or another (even a quick hurried trip to the loo). Grab some water and something to eat, then drop one off at music lessons, a quick trip back home or to the shops to pick up something for dinner. Then drop the second child off for netball training, back to pick up my youngest from day-care, then back to pick up the one at music lessons and then back home to get dinner on, then out again to pick up the last from netball training'.

It was a manic time, and somewhere in between I was also studying for a master's degree. I would be up at 5am to get a few hours of study in before the family rose from their beds to greet another day. After dinner was cleared at night and children tucked away in their beds, then I would hit the books again. But only after the kids had finished doing their homework, doing another load of washing and getting school lunches ready for the next day. It was a lot to take on with no family around to help me as we moved to Queensland and all the family support was in Sydney. Plus, in and around all this madness I worked work 32 hours a week for a community agency.

Somehow, it 'had to be' and I just soldiered on. In 1997 my husband was made redundant. In some ways this was a hard time, living on my earnings from my part time job. But, in many ways it was a blessing. With hubby at home and out of work, he could do some of the Mum's Taxi work. He took the time to upgrade his qualifications during this time and to supplement our income he took up some horrid jobs like chicken catching, cleaning poop from chicken barns out. I remember one day he came home and stripped his clothing at the door as he was covered in poop from head to toe. He did this as we needed the extra money to pay for school fees. If it has got to be, you do anything.

Whilst those times were really hard financially, but with Dad at home it took the pressure off us both. Eventually hubby graduated and landed the job of a lifetime. That time was also a good example to our children that education was an asset, and you constantly need to study and upgrade your skills.

In 1999, my husband's sister invited us to her wedding, in England. We had never visited them as it was very expensive to travel. We wanted his family to meet all our children, so again Patt's words rang in my ears. We held a family meeting and decided 'YES, we want to go' was the resounding answer from the family. So, we made a plan and save, save, save!

We cut back things like having any take-away food, the best we had for months was hot chips. We stopped hiring videos on Friday and Saturday nights (no streaming services then). We bought generic food and ate lots of veggies and fruit. We would turn off every light to keep the bill low. By this time two of our children had found part time jobs. This meant more 'flying about' for the trusty old Bluebird car.

We had a picture of a 'thermometer' on the fridge and had turns in colouring in growth in our savings every month. We would collect twenty percent of the kid's income and bank this into a special bank account set up for our holiday. Even our youngest child of 11yo did a paper round. Mind you, all of family would be involved in folding papers and inserting brochures which were deliver to homes in the local area. We did this horrid job for almost nine months, but everything added up.

The day came that we had saved up enough to book airfares. It was exciting to finally do this. Then we saved harder for spending money and new clothes. We finally went on our holiday. At that time, it took three Australian dollars to gain one English pound. We did a budget, rarely ate out, although who can resist a nice Sunday roast at an English pub. We picked up 5-pound return tickets to Calais, France. This led to an impromptu trip to Paris and back to Calais as the tickets only last 24 hours. We made it on the last Ferry, but it was a fun trip. And because we planned things we even came back to Australia with spare money and bought a new computer.

I think our children learned a lot from our England wedding holiday. They learned that if they want something, education, travel etc, it takes planning and hard work to achieve any goal. We often laugh about the trip to Paris in 2000.

In 2002 I was diagnosed with invasive breast cancer. This happened around the beginning of March. I was 44yo at that time.

How did it all start. Well, I found a small pea like lump whilst in the shower. I kept touching this lump. A bit like how you get something stuck in your teeth. At first, I thought that the lump was maybe a blind pimple and tried to squeeze it. But nothing came out. Using an 'old wives' tale' method, I put a Band-Aid on the lump and left it on for a few days thinking it would draw any toxins to a head. But nothing changed. The lump was still there. I didn't go to my doctors for about 10 days as I already had an appointment booked. As soon as my doctor felt the lump, he asked his Receptionist to make me an appointment for a breast screen test.

You kind of get the inkling that something might be serious when your doctor takes urgent action. Similarly, you also know something isn't right when staff at the breast screen centre call you back in twice to get more images.

I vividly still recall the time that the radiology Doctor came in to tell me the news that as well as the lump I found, there were 3 more lumps against the chest muscle wall. She went on to add that she had already made an appointment for me to have a conical biopsy at the Mater Hospital the next day to confirm what the lumps were made of.

Well, tests revealed that I had two types of breast cancer in one breast. I was given an emergency referral to see a specialist breast surgeon later that week. Anyone who has had a diagnosis of a severe illness knows that feeling at being told 'you have cancer', or some other acute illness. Your mind just runs wild after you receive that news.

I recall that the language around my diagnosis also started to change. At first the word of 'lump' was used, then came the word 'tumours' and not just 1 but multiple aggressive tumours. Doesn't a diagnosis of cancer and tumours mean a death warrant.

Again, Patt's words were in my head.

The day came to see the surgeon. Various options were laid out by the surgeon. With lots of support from hubby and my family I decided to take the most radical of options of a full mastectomy. This meant a 6-hour operation to remove my left breast and surrounding lymph nodes under my armpit. The operation was scheduled for 5 days later.

I remember how I felt the day I was admitted. I remember thinking to myself: "Well lady, there's no point looking back. Your best chance of survival means losing a breast. If it had to be, it's got to be!'. A bit like how you feel when you have a tooth removed.

The surgery went well. Samples of the lumps were sent off to pathology which confirmed the type of breast cancer. The other news was mixed. First the good news; 'The tumours had not vesiculated to the chest wall, so removal was clean and no damage to the heart'. First time I knew about that risk! The downside was that it had spread to one (1) lymph node.

The day after the surgery, a specialist oncologist came to visit me to introduce himself and to advise that I would have a formal meeting with him around 10 days later to discussion options. It was a harrowing time with much to take in.

I met the Oncologist who outlined treatment options and risks. Again, I agreed to have the strongest of treatments and if my body could not tolerate things, I could drop levels of treatment, but this also increased risk of reoccurrence. I recall asking the Oncologist about my prognosis. He said 'Well, I will put it this way. If you get through one year then you might have a good chance of another and hopefully another'. I underwent nine (9) months of chemotherapy for hormone reactive breast cancer, and three (3) more operations.

In 2003 I was referred to a plastic surgeon to discuss having a procedure called a 'Tram flap breast reconstruction'. This is an operation to 'create' a new breast using my own tissue. This involves removal of the lower four core muscles and transplant the muscle and skin to create a new breast. That operation went generally well, only a couple of minor issue. Later I had two more operations to reduce the size of my right breast and create a sort of nipple shape. I looked horrendous for 5 months, but eventually the surgery settled.

I continued seeing the Oncologist for 2 years and the breast surgeon for another 9 years as during my time with the breast surgeon I was registered to participate in a long-term clinical trial in the use of hormone blocker medication called 'Tamoxifen'. I participated in this clinical trial for 11 years and 5 months and was declared a success. The day came when the breast surgeon advised that I was being discharged and advised go off and life my life... Cancer free.

I joined a local breast cancer support group and met a lady called Edith Cooper. She was giving a talk about her recent trip to China with a breast cancer dragon boat team in Brisbane called 'Missabittatitti'. I loved the team's name and she encouraged me to come along to a trial come and try day. The team paddle on the Brisbane River two to three times a week. After one session I was hooked! The team would often paddle on Tuesday or Thursday mornings too. I was pretty dedicated and would paddle early, then go to work to shower before starting my workday.

The whole club of Missabittatitti was made up of breast cancer survivors and a few supporters. In 2005, news was released that the next International Breast Cancer Paddling Commission Festival Regatta would be held in Kawana, Queensland. The gauntlet was laid, and I WANTED to be there.

Again, Pat's words were in my head. If I was to survive and paddle in the international regatta then I would have to work at it. I trained three to four (3-4) times a week. I joined my first gym and for the first time I put my interests first, not after needs of the family.

The hard work paid off and I was included into the 'A' team and our club won the major plate. In fact, the second team also won the minor plate. It was an amazing event with breast cancer teams and individual competitors coming from all over the world. I had my medal mounted and proudly displays in my home study.

After the Festival was over, I decided that I wanted to help my team grow. Over the years our club has competed in various competitions around Australia, at state sports paddle regattas held around Australia, plus international breast cancer regatta festivals in Peterborough, Canada in 2010, Hong Kong in 2012 and Sarasota, USA in 2014 and more.

After the international event in Sarasota, Florida in 2014 I was elected to the position of Club Coordinator, a role similar to that of a club president. I felt confident I could bring the skills I had from my professional job, studies and experience as a paddler together and work with the Committee to improve club operations and growth of the club.

A key challenge was participating in the 55km Ord River Paddle Challenge. This event is held annually by the local dragon boat club at Kununurra in Western Australia. The endurance paddle starts at the spill gate of the Lake Argyle dam wall. Dam operators release water downstream. Teams then paddle special steel dragon boats from the dam's spill way down the Ord River all the way to the town of Kununurra.

This is a huge paddle and the team invested even more time training for long periods on the Brisbane River in preparation for the endurance paddle. The paddle was tough going in parts as we paddled through rapids from the release of dam water and croc infested territory, but we made it. It is one of my biggest achievements, along with winning the AIA race at Caloundra in 2007 and trekking into Machu Picchu!

Sadly, I did not see out my term as President as shortly after the endurance paddle was held, I became ill with what seemed like a common cold. I had extreme difficulty breathing with what I thought was just a flu or asthma. After blacking out I called the Ambulance as my husband was on night shift. I couldn't talk, I could barely gasp any air. The Ambulance officer on the phone made me press buttons on the phone to locate where I was. Soon they arrived and I was rushed to Redland's hospital. On arrival the emergency doctor (her name was Nancy) did a blood test.

Shortly afterwards I was wheeled into a private room. All the nurses and doctors who came after that all wore gowns and masks. I didn't know it until my hubby arrived, but there was a stream of tape across my door 'Do Not Enter'.

At last, the Senior Registrar came into see us. He advised that I was going to be transferred by to the major regional hospital: Princess Alexandra Hospital or more commonly known locally in Brisbane as the 'P.A.' to have more tests.

On arrival at the hospital in the ambulance, a woman called out to the Ambulance Officer, "Is that the transfer from Redlands with 'Acute Myeloid Leukaemia?" What the!!

I immediately turned to the Ambulance staff and asked was the lady shouting out about me. The officer named Gary said "Yes, you are one very sick lady". I was in shock. My only experience related to Leukaemia as far as I knew was that it was akin to a death sentence.

I did not sleep a wink that night as my mind was racing, and no laptop around to reach for 'Doctor Google' to help me gain information.

After this I underwent numerous tests including a sampling of bone marrow from my hip bone. The next day all the medical team all entered my room. In came seven people, the senior specialist haematology and oncology doctor, the resident haematologist and oncologist doctor, the trainee haematology and ward registrar doctor, the clinical leukaemia nurse, the ward nurse, the social worker and the family advocate from the Leukaemia Foundation. My small room was packed with all these people wearing masks, and this was long before Covid situation where the wearing of masks now is very common. At that time, it was scary.

My husband was also required to be present. As my immediate carer it was explained that he needed to be present to receive the news.

The Senior haematology and oncology doctor advised that bone marrow samples and other blood tests all confirmed earlier results: I had blood cancer! And worse still one of the worst kinds; Acute Myeloid Leukaemia (also known as 'AML').

The doctor advised that I was already neutropenic. We had to ask what that meant. They explained that my body was not producing white blood cells and more importantly neutrophils, so I had nothing in my body to fight off any infection. Test revealed I had 1 neutrophil which was fighting hard, but I needed an army of neutrophils.

Doctors explained that this was the reason why I was placed into an isolation ward and why anyone who came to visit, even medical staff, all were required wear surgical masks at all times whilst in my room. They advised that in addition all visitors would need to put on plastic gowns and gloves before coming into my room.

In addition, they advised that I was also critically low in red blood cells. This meant that I would need urgent transfusions of blood and platelets to 'feed' my body as my bone marrow had stopped making blast cells to make these items. It was explained that transfusions only 'top up' the body and that this was not a long-term option. My only option was to first boost my blood work, then attack benign cells being created by the blood cancer with very heavy duty chemotherapy treatment. This treatment they advised was 10 times strong than the chemo I had for breast cancer. They explained that I would need this treatment in 3 stages. Stage 1 would commence at the end of the week and would involve 250 hours of continuous infusion of chemo drugs.

Whoa... 250 hours! After this initial treatment more tests would be undertaken. If results were good, and after my body started producing normal red and white blood cells, then I would need another 250 hours in about 6-8 weeks' time, with the same routine occurring after that. It takes 6-8 weeks for the body to build up stocks of red and white blood cells. There were lots more discussion and many questions. The Treatment Team answered most.

But there was more bad news. The senior doctor then advised that patients with AML do not recover from use of chemo alone and the chance for reoccurrence and death was high. It was explained that this form of leukaemia only has a long-term success when patients undergo a stem cell or bone marrow transplant.

A TRANSPLANT! What the Xxxx.

Both my hubby's and my head were spinning with this news. It was explained that all my siblings would be tested to see if any were a match and if not, the team would search the world-wide marrow register to try and find someone with the same blood and gene type.

After more discussions and questions, the clinical nurse presented us with numerous documents to read and sign. The first thing done was completion of the consent to start emergency blood transfusions and undergo various other invasive tests. Once my blood levels were up, then I would need to sign the consent to start chemotherapy treatment.

Again, Patt's words bounced back into my head, in fact they screamed at me:

IF IT HAS GOT TO BE… THEN IT IS UP TO ME!

Her words kept repeating in my head.   The reality was, I was a very sick person with few choices. I could undergo treatment as per the care plan and hope like hell that a cell match could be found via my siblings with the thin chance of getting to the transplant stage, or, do nothing.

Hubby asked if I wanted more time to think about things. I looked at him, shook my head and said to the Care Team; 'Okay. Give me both barrels and full on. Who has a pen so I can sign the dotted line?' The medical team all seemed relieved with my response.   Through tears I signed the paperwork.

After the care team left, my husband gave me the more heavenly hug. I could feel his fear. It was such a warm embrace. We decided that we wanted to advise our three daughters first. He then went outside to ring our three (3) children. All of them came to visit me that night. We cried, we hugged, and cried again. Between us, we called my brothers and sisters. They needed to know the news so we could start conversations about being tested as a possible bone marrow or stem cell donor.

How I wished that my parents were still alive. I needed to talk to my Mum!

During the visit from all our daughters we discussed who they could talk to about my leukaemia news. One of my daughters asked if they could post anything to social media. I sat for a moment to think and said; 'No point keeping this a secret. By the sound of things, I might be in here (hospital) for a long time.' I remember saying; 'You lot have probably already told your hubbies and partners, maybe even the grandies.' Gently pointing to one even the daughter. 'I know you must have already told the other grand-parents as they are looking after your kids tonight so you can be here. So, maybe it is best that we just post something on Facebook. That way, all of you don't have to have many difficult conversations or respond to texts.'

We all agreed. We took a family photo with everyone wearing their masks bar me and posted this news up on Facebook. Using social media to communicate the news was probably one of the best things we did. I had a large circle of family, personal and professional contacts. I knew that the post would reach most of our family, friends and work colleagues who lived in many parts of Australia. It worked and quickly too. Soon we had contact from many of our extended family and friends even those who lived overseas.

My husband and daughters stayed for a while and we chatted about all sorts of things. One daughter who was a nurse noted that I looked tired. Yes, I was exhausted. It had been a huge day with lots of information to process. I was running on empty with very low blood counts and did need to rest. The family decided that they had not eaten either and decided to go off and find somewhere for dinner. In a way, I was sad to see them go, but also shed a sigh of relief. I did need to rest, but more importantly I needed time to myself just to reflect on the tough road ahead of me. Would I survive? Didn't blood cancer mean a death sentence?

As many who have had long periods of hospitalisation, you soon realise that hospital life does not allow patients much time to rest. Nursing staff buzzed in and out every 3 hours to take observation tests, dispense medication, take blood for more tests or change IV bags. Other staff stopped into wheel in equipment, deliver paperwork and of course meals.

I remember that I was really tired, but just couldn't sleep. My head was racing with all that information. I must have picked up and read the information that was provided about Acute Myeloid Leukaemia several times through. How I wish I had my trusty laptop, so I research more information!

I had my phone which started buzzing with texts and phone calls. It got so bad that I turned the phone to silent. Too much to process and I didn't have the energy.

After some time, my mind started to settle. I remember saying to myself; 'Look at the positives. I had a care plan. I was in a good hospital. I had been through chemo and treatment for breast cancer before so had some idea of what was ahead of me.

I had to do this and put faith in the medical team that their care plan would give me the best chance of survival'. And Patt's words were back: 'If it has got to be, it has to be'. The night nurse popped in. More observations. I asked for something to help me sleep. She said she would talk to the doctor. Around twenty (20) minutes later she returned with a sleeping tablet. I took the tablet straight away, but it still took some time to drift off to sleep. Sleep eventually came until 4.50am when another nurse came in to take morning blood tests. As I said, hospitals are no place to sleep!

The next day was busy, new nurses, more blood tests. Later in the morning the transfusions of blood and platelet were started, and yes, more tests. This went on for about 10 days. Then the first chemotherapy treatment day arrived. Gasp! I dreaded the thought of having two hundred and fifty hours (250) of continuous chemotherapy drugs being pumped into my body. I had to tell myself over and over that even though chemotherapy is technically poison, I needed it to get well again. In came the clinical nurse to oversee the start of the new chemo treatment. He advised that this concoction of poison was ten times more lethal than the chemo I had for breast cancer. Gasp! But did add that anti-nausea medications had improved so this would help me get through treatment. They did, but I won't lie, the treatment was still pretty tough going.

In the same week as my first chemotherapy treatment, the location of the next international breast cancer paddling festival was announced. It was a bit like the Olympics when they announce the next host country. And the winner is…. Florence, Italy.

I decided then and there, I was going to get well enough to get to fly to Florence and paddle in the international festival.

Every day I had tests and blood samples were taken. After the first 250 hours of chemo infusion was over, I was kept in the isolation room for around 8 weeks. The numbers of visitors that I could have was strictly limited and monitored. As to any gifts they could bring. I couldn't have any flowers or plants, these have bacteria. I could not see my grand-children and anyone coming to visit still had to mask and gown up, stay 1 mitre away from me and definitely no kissing or hugging. But I did break that rule a few times.

After news about Florence being named as the next international paddling festival location, my daughter brought in a picture of the Duomo Cathedral which is a central tourist interest in Florence. She pinned this photograph of the Duomo dome on the pin board on the wall at the end of my bed. She said to me 'Now Mum, your challenge is to get well enough to go to Florence'. Her words became part a personal mantra and I would repeat these words to myself hundreds of times a day 'Get Well, Get to Florence!'

After the first round of two hundred and fifty hours of chemo was passed, I had to endure nine weeks of rehabilitation. Twice a day I had blood tests. Every morning you anxiously await arrival of the medical registrar to give you results as to whether any neutrophils were emerging. You see medical staff can give you blood type and platelet transfusions, but the one thing they cannot give you is white blood cells. These are developed by your body and can only be used by the owner. Another person's white cells can't work. Finally, the day came when the medical registrar came into my room and did a happy dance. No words. I knew what that meant. I had to wait another five weeks until levels were at 'usual levels' and I was finally allowed to go home for a 10-day break before starting the phase of treatment.

I remember leaving the hospital early September. I can remember the teel of the touch of sunline on my face as we drove along. I felt like a freed bird.

Unfortunately, my freedom was short lived. After just 5 days, I was readmitted due to very high infection. Back to hospital I go and strangely, back to the same room that I had left not long ago. Once again, more tests to find the root cause of the infection. As my temperature was so high, the medical team prescribed an immediate infusion of three strains of anti-biotics in the hope that one of the medications would kill bacteria my system was fighting. The next forty-eight (48) hours was critical. My body was in a lather of sweat. The family were gathered around as doctors advised that things were 'touch and go'.

I briefly recall a visit from a very dear friend. I was fading in and out. I heard my hubby say that I may never be able to travel overseas. On hearing those words, I said; 'Oh yes, I will. I am going to fight this and keep fighting. I pulled through. A lesson hard learned. I couldn't eat some of my favourite foods, at least for a while.

After I head beaten the gremlins off, I started the next round of 250 hours of chemo about ten days later. Patt's words are back again. If it has got to be.. it is up to me!

During all this time, my siblings had all been contacted by staff from the hospital haematology department. I was very lucky to have come from a family which six children.

All give siblings were given the opportunity to be tested as a possible donor. Four travelled at different times to Brisbane to get tested. The fifth, was tested close to where he lived. Finally test results arrived. I remember that day so clearly. Doctors advised that my younger sister's genome and blood type was a suitable cell match and that it looked likely that I would not need a donation off the international register.

This news was like winning the lottery. Whilst the news that my sister's cells were a match, this did not guarantee that I would get into the transplant program. Both my sister had to undergo a series of tests and it was not until result were examined by the transplant clinic would we know if further treatment was possible.

During the wait period my hubby and daughter attended a workshop provided by the Leukaemia Foundation. It was entitled 'The Nuts and Bolts of Transplants'. They were so energised by the possibilities that they left the workshop early and came to visit me. Their energy at entering my ward was amazing. They were full of hope and kept talking about the research work of a Professor Hill who was actually located in Brisbane.

Finally, news was delivered by the Leukaemia Clinical Nurse that the Transplant Clinic at Royal Brisbane and Women's Hospital had reviewed all results for my sister and myself and that we will be advised of an initial appointment to meet with the Transplant Tea. About twenty minutes after this meeting the Clinical Nurse came into report that my case was being taken up by Professor Hill. We were overjoyed at this news.

Professor Hill had agreed to meet with us to discuss a possible transplant of cells or marrow from my sister. The day came for the meeting. Hubby and I were both very nervous as we formally had not been accepted. After preliminary discussions were had, Professor Hill asked what exercise I did. I explained that I was a dragon boat paddler. I told him about the 55km endurance paddle I had completed just three weeks prior to my initial diagnosis. He said 'Well, if you were strong enough to do that, then you should have a good chance of surviving a transplant.'

I was accepted to the Transplant program. The program is multi-layered and meant more tests, more chemotherapy treatment and yes, there were risks. Huge risks! I didn't care about having more chemo or treatment. I just said, 'bring it on'. If these procedures provided a great chance of longer life, then 'If it has meant to be, it is up to me'.

Patt's words jumped out again and again to help me to move on to next phase.

I had a big goal ahead of me – life. The possibility of travelling to Florence was starting to feel real.

We felt like we had won the lottery! A lottery to save my life.

After the meeting with Professor Hill, we then met with the Transplant Coordination team who got to the task of organizing a whole range of tests for my sister and I.

My sister lived interstate. She was flown to Brisbane two times to have additional tests. Leading up to Transplant Day or 'T-Day', my sister had to learn how to inject herself with a substance to promote growth of stem cells. This was done on a daily basis.

After six (6) days of self-injection my sister was flown to Brisbane again. She was admitted to Level 4 of the hospital. I had been admitted three days before to start pre-transplant treatment. My new home at the hospital was in a special pressure sealed room located on Gasp! Level 5. So, we could not see each other.

On the day before transplant, my sister sat for seven (7) hours whilst doctors collected (sometimes referred to as being 'harvest'), precious stem cells. The official name of the procedure is called 'apheresis'.

On the same day I underwent a final and life-threatening round of more chemotherapy. Patients are advised that many don't survive this final round as it virtually kills off patients' cells in readiness to receive the donated stem cells or bone marrow.

Stem Cell Transplant treatments are preferred these days over bone marrow as the process has the same outcome without invasive surgery to both the donor and leukaemia patient.

On the morning of 22nd October, 2015, I kept saying to myself the following two mantras:

'If it has got to be.. then it is up to me'

and

'Live for Graham (hubby), Get to Florence'
and not necessarily in that order.

I must have said the above words to myself thousands and thousands of times. Prior to the transplant I tried to fill my mind by reading or research on the internet everything I could about Florence: the history, the museums, tours and travel plans. I even started learning the Italian language via an online service. I would set myself a daily reminder to complete an Italian class language and try to listen to music or the news spoken or sung in Italian to try and learn more of the language. Italians talk fast! I continued this practice for almost two years.

The next eight (8) months post the receiving my sister's cells was a blur. During the first month post-transplant I was accommodated in a special ward and another isolation room with negative pressure air-conditioning. The room was fitted out with all sorts of equipment and nursing supplies. For the first week you are treated like an ICU patient with round the clock care and daily tests, sometimes two or three times a day, for this or that.

I won't lie, treatment leading up to the transplant and the post-transplant process was tough. Very tough at times. You are constantly nauseous. Your body is fighting off a foreign element, everything you touch or eat has potential for bacteria. This means more infusions of anti-biotics, blood, plasma or other things. Utensils had to be sterile, Food had to be fresh, and fruit and vegetables needed to be washed three times and cooked fresh. I could not eat any frozen food, take-away food apart from food cooked in boiling oil fryers. Apparently, no bacteria can withstand that level of heat.

Gradually things got easier with the help of anti-rejection and anti-nausea and many other medications. The first morning after transplant the nurse came in with new daily medications for me to take. I gasped at the number of pills. I needed to take 21 tablets morning and night. Talk about a spoon full of sugar to make the medicine go down. I needed a jug full.

Once discharged from hospital, you don't get to stay home. No, every day we were back at the Leukaemia Clinic initially for blood tests, then to see the haematology doctors, then to stay and wait for more blood transfusion or other treatments. It was like going to work, only this time the work was all about saving your life.

We were advised by the Transplant Coordinator that the cost of Treatment was around $400,000. Having been through it, I do not doubt what she said. So many doctors, tests, medications, procedures, treatments. I give thanks every day to the wonderful medical care I have had.

With the help of my husband, family, work mates and family I started the slow recovery process

On the anniversary of my first-year post-transplant I commenced a 'Thrive to Survive' exercise program. This program is funded by a philanthropist and provided by the Leukaemia Foundation. The exercises are basic, but it was explained that a year of living in hospitals and rehabilitation at home, my muscles had weakened. I had to start strengthening everything just like a newborn baby needs to learn to roll and crawl before they can walk.

After another six months of rehabilitation, I returned to paddling and my sister who donated cells and I paddled in a race together at Darling Harbour. It didn't matter that our team didn't win… we were both winners just paddling side by side with many other breast cancer warrior women. And did I return to work? I sure did, but to a different role.

Did I get to paddle in Florence? I sure did. A very proud moment on many levels. I finally got to speak some Italian. I recall that we went out for dinner and I successfully organised a table, order of wine, sorting out the bill and more.

Our team trained three to four times a week. I was selected to Team A and our team won our first heat at the international festival regatta.

After the race was finished teams, all give three cheers to the other teams. A comradery thing. On completion of the 3 cheers, I burst into tears. It hit me that I had survived the transplant, had become strong enough to paddle here at the international festival in Florence. Here I was sitting in the boat with my team members on the Arno River. It was great that we won our first heat, but for me arriving at that moment was special and still brings joy today.

My husband and sister both travelled to Florence. They also participated in the parade of nations with my team and all the international teams who marched across the Ponte Vecchio Bridge to the opening ceremonies in the Republica Square. This event was attended by thousands of participants from one hundred and thirty-five (135) teams from thirty-nine (39) countries. They also paddled on the Arno River in the supporter category boat.

I survived all that treatment and many other difficult situations in life, all thanks to the special words of advice which I received from an important mentor: Patt Smith. Her advice encouraged me to go complete higher education, gain employment and promotions at work, move states for hubbie's work, handle difficult family situations and lots more.

I have survived a scare of cervical cancer in 1996, breast cancer and breast removal and reconstructive plastic surgery in 2002 & 2003 respectively. I had lip cancer and reconstructive plastic surgery to remove one third of my lower lip in 2009, then blood cancer and a transplant in 2015. I have had amazing care from health professionals and support from my family.

Yes, I have been through a bloody lot.

Next year will be 20 years since the words – you have breast cancer was formally said and the advice from the Oncologist to 'get through one year and you may have another' was also received. So, will I get to the next international festival to be held in New Zealand? I sure will be working hard to get there.

IF IT HAS GOT TO BE... THEN IT IS UP TO ME!

So, the moral of my story - If you are faced with tough or difficult situation like adverse health news, a tough work assignment or any other tough thing in your life, then don't give up or give in. If it is important to you, determine what you want, give yourself goals, make a plan, stay positive and crack on. And if you fail first time, do like my Nan said; 'Try, Try, and Try again'.

One last thing.. below are the words to our paddle club's team song. It is sung to the tune of 'Hokey Pokey'...

> You put what's left in,
>
> You put what's left out,
>
> You put what's left in and shake it all about
>
> We are "Missabittatitti' and we turn things around
>
> That's what we're all about!
>
> Oh   Missabittatitti,   Oohh   Missabittatitti,   Ooohhh Missabittattitti
>
> Paddling is what we are all about! Oi!

I hope my story inspires others.

Janelle Pritchard
Retired Multiple Cancer Survivor (previously a Business Systems (Quality and Risk Manager) for a national charity.

Picture this. She's an 'alone' child. Not lonely, because she has her imagination and uses it. But she's always alone. She is loved, but she doesn't know she is because she's never told. In fact, she lacks confidence because she feels she's not valued. Thankfully, she believes in her heart she has value. She knows she's a good girl, and she certainly has desires and passions. She has little in common with her siblings, so there is no comfort from those relationships. Her mother suffers from depression, which manifests in words of anger and frustration, so the 'alone' child either stays out of the way or seeks approval. She's intelligent but not skilled at sharp retorts in response to slights by others. What can she do? She could go inside herself; forever resigned to not achieving to her potential or she could chase those desires and passions. She chooses the latter. Slowly, slowly, she ventures out of her comfort zone. One step forward, two steps back. She doesn't want to step on toes; she knows how it feels to be stepped on. So, she accomplishes slowly, purposefully. She's frequently paralysed by fear. Fear of rejection, fear of put-downs and fear of being perceived as entitled. She learns to 'feel the fear and do it, anyway'. She learns to shine. You can too. You can.

Rhonda Valentine Dixon

Confront fear with preparation.

Many times, in life when I needed to approach a daunting task or enter a new or different situation I would be crippled with fear. I'd put things off, avoid them or simply walk the other way. Something as simple as making a phone call for a job interview, making a complaint to a government department or boss was difficult. Maybe it was not knowing what to do, getting the wording wrong or fear of confrontation.

I remember starting a new job in the late 80's at a TV production company and was super 'stressed out' about deadlines, keeping clients happy and making mistakes. Again, when I worked in the computer games industry as a 3D artist I thought to myself 'I can't do this!... and do I really want to!' It was at both these companies that I discovered my go to strategy for dealing with work-related fear and anxiety. The key was preparation.

Before I started any new job or task I would look for as much reference, research and art examples as I could. I was prepared. I was 'studied'. I was 'armed'. Later when I worked as a teacher in video production and finally on my first feature film, again, preparation and planning was key. Amidst the day to day chaos of film production or teaching at least I was pretty sure of one thing... 'any plan, and strategy is better than no plan at all'. Some accused me of being too prepared, be it worked for me.

A simple computer game analogy: You are playing an RTS and you build up your forces to a ridiculous capacity before attacking. Over time, and through attrition your enemy has weakened and sometimes attack is even unnecessary if you arrive as ready as possible.

Practice being prepared or even over prepared... and see where it gets you.

Brian Vining, Film maker and Teacher

Perseverance

Sometimes in life you struggle and find daily living is a challenge.

Never give up!

Some problems are transitory, and you can get through them with perseverance.

Have confidence that your struggles will pay off in the long run.

Ian

"Out of your Head & into your heart…"

The beauty most definitely lies within.. our job is to trust & have faith to follow the divine energy flowing into our heart so we can be the change in the World we need to see!

Have you ever felt overwhelmed, tired, worn out, no longer fulfilled & questioning what you are doing & how long you can continue?
Yes… me too! I know how you feel as I felt the same way!
I was at a crossroad after having our third child whilst on maternity leave & dragging my feet to head back to my career!
You see, up until that time I served my Country as an Aircraft Maintenance Engineer in the Royal Australian Air Force for 17 years & was so blessed to have been given so many incredible experiences others might never & was also blessed to have been part of an incredible military family, having friends all around Australia as a result but I remember there was a time when I just woke up, my soul was being stirred & thought, "how could I continue this ego driven career, having someone else raise our children, working extra-long hours & for what? "

I was told years prior that as a female I couldn't carry out that career, so I said, "move over & watch this space!" I proved I was more than capable! I learnt that other people's opinions of you have nothing to do with you and everything to do with their own fears!
I was blessed to have met my wonderful husband of almost 27 years on the tarmac …yes just like a Top Gun Romance, but, I was now at the top of the ceiling of my expertise & without goals & what I thought …no opportunities of progress.. it no longer fulfilled or lit me up … So, I knew something had to change! I just had no idea, how or what & nor did I need to know! During the time off with my new little baby…the GIFT I now see, was TIME & SPACE!

I really had no idea why this was so important & the gift it would be in my life, but didn't question & chose to use the time to carry out daily meditation, visualizing, grounding myself out in nature, carrying out my morning rituals and affirmations as well as concentrating on breathing exercises & the importance of this..

I now know I was divinely lead as this would lead me to tuning in & not dismissing my heart & using my intuition as my inner GPS when I most needed whilst smashing that voice in my head I had been so accustomed to as an Engineer... Thank goodness!

This would allow me to see that everything I needed is already inside, instead of giving my power away & looking elsewhere!

This would allow me to manifest more profoundly as I could see just how to bring my dreams into reality but also I now know that as much as you can manifest good things, you can also manifest tragedies....things sent to truly awaken you & ensure you tune into your heart space & this is something many Law of attraction experts do not share!

You see ...what I know is the Universe, higher power, your subconscious or whatever you'd like to call it, always rewards what you ask for, so you have to be careful what you ask for!

And that, sadly is with everything in life.. You have to carefully look at your life & understand that where you are right now is a result of all of your choices as we are the biggest creators so even when obstacles show up, you have to tune in and ask what you need to learn by that obstacle and what need it fulfilled by you creating it.... Once you truly understand that, you can then use that to the best of your knowledge as you grow & continue to evolve throughout your life as things are always happening for and not to you! Sometimes can be hard lessons and totally hard to understand.. trust me.. I have been there but as you grow and evolve and see the beauty, you grow to understand that perhaps you were chosen to have these obstacles show up to reveal more of yourself and build more strength and resilience as you are powerful & it better prepares you for what is to come as there is not a day that goes by and we do not have a learning experience..

At times, we might question and yes you do need time to truly feel the pain but we need to understand that nothing is permanent, only our souls & we can overcome anything sent our way & learn the lesson as this time too shall pass! And... as much as your heart gives you what you ask for.. if you choose to not listen and instead tune into your head.. You may never have the freedom & excitement as your head is designed to keep you safe and in your comfort zone!

By smashing that voice and doing the work to tune into your heart.. that is where the beauty lies and where you then start really living & this is a choice for you to decide! Energy grows where energy flows! That has been a very big lesson to learn and understand! Going back to that day where I truly woke up and was given the gift of tuning into my heart, leading up to that time.. you see.. I did ask for change but had no idea how it would come to me & never, not for a million years did I expect a full-on tragedy to wake me up & that is the lesson & what needs to be shared!

Never did I expect to have every parent's worst nightmare to suddenly become my reality? I am a good Mum that always puts her children first! So... Never did I expect to find our little baby boy, the only one left in my care, the one I was to look after & protect, fully clothed including shoes and a nappy, floating in our backyard pool on my watch!

It still horrifies and haunts me to this day!

I still tear up to this day!

But it happened! And... even though it was full-on to go through and I do not recommend for anyone to have to experience.. it gave me what I asked for... It gave me a chance to be reignited, to get out of the status quo, to come alive again, to see unlimited possibilities everywhere, to get excited on just who I am going to meet on a daily basis because of this newfound energy I discovered & most importantly it gave me a purpose so my life could have true meaning and I could leave a legacy, well after I left!

Fortunately... I now see my life as a dot to dot & see the reason why I was so divinely lead to focus on the rituals so I could not dismiss that pushing feeling coming from my intuition, despite my mind trying to tell me he was ok & would be playing with his toys in another room! Thank goodness I couldn't dismiss that calling!

So blessed! This all happened on what was meant to be the most exciting day! The day we were moving into our first home we purchased! The day, my husband was at the Hardware Store ironically buying child locks to ensure our home was safe... the day, he was our only child in my care as a baby.. The day I was busy unpacking boxes as my little baby boy was placed in my site & never use to wander off and explore!

The day, I was complacent & just assumed my pool gate would have been checked by my Building Inspector upon purchase of our property! There are many lessons I have learnt during this experience.. one very big one is to NEVER ASSUME! I run over and over the events of that day & question why and how did this happen & why I did not hear a splash or a scream whilst being busy that day?

And every single day, I am so grateful for the time leading up to this day…the day where my life changed FOREVER!

You see…

I could not dismiss the calling & despite running from room to room & box to box searching, I knew, deep down inside me that it was the pool… I just did not want to believe it! I saw it and actually visualised it, but still was trying to not believe.. to ignore the pain in my heart! So when I took those steps to our pool and my vision became my reality… I screamed uncontrollably for someone to come and help, however no one was home, neighbours were all out as well! As I nervously reached into the pool to pull out his lifeless body, screaming, I raced inside to try and call emergency on my home phone that wasn't even connected!

Everything I was trying was failing me! I remember thinking very clearly…how could I call my husband and other daughters to advise them that our little bundle of joy… the one we tried for so much, was no longer with us? It could not be in my equation! My God.. I was a mess and could not stop shaking! I had to try and find my mobile phone to make the call but as I frantically went searching for it…I had a divine energy or force come over me, telling me to get over myself… that this was not about me, but about him & if I didn't try something, anything… he would no longer be in our lives!

How often in life do we not do things or delay because we don't feel good enough or it's not perfect? This, I had to get over & as I breathed deep that caused me to realise I had to just try something & it didn't need to be PERFECT another powerful lesson! Psychologists have carried out studies about the effects of deep breathing during traumas… it allows you to get out of the emotion and into a clinical approach during tragedies.. I didn't know that at the time, but again…

his time wasn't up & I was divinely led to do just that without question!
I lay his little lifeless body down, carried out one rotation, which by no means was not perfect & nothing happened, but I continued and on the second rotation.... he started breathing!!! I could not believe it! I was truly blessed! I then found my mobile phone and made the call and waited 15 minutes for Paramedics to arrive so had to keep him alive that time that felt like a lifetime! Our baby... me... we were given another shot at life! Tears streaming down my face of sheer gratitude!

I am not a hero.. I am a Mum that was truly blessed to be given some incredible tools to help save my son! What I now know is just how easily unplanned incidents can occur & just how 20 seconds can change your life forever! Paramedics could not believe he was alive as sadly most immersion incidents like this, result in loss of life & so upon arrival, they were overcome by emotions and embraced me as tears streamed from us all! It was such a powerful moment!

And yet again.. another powerful incident where I learnt some pretty full on lessons that NEED to be shared by being my authentic self and so relatable, coming directly from my heart! They knew my story was powerful and needed to be shared and if we could reach even one person and they could learn from this horrific story, our mission would be accomplished! They immediately immersed me into the media in an attempt to share my story in an attempt for others to learn & better protect their loved ones! I just knew that was the change I had been asking for... in the form of a tragedy to wake me up, to see my gifts and show me the unlimited possibilities by tuning into my heart & having faith to follow the divine energy every single day! What a way to wake up!!

And once again.. I do not recommend this story for you to wake up as there most certainly are other ways in which I did learn through this experience to truly help you live a life you deserve! Yes at that moment.. it changed me forever as with the help of the media & my absolute desire to scream this Story & the many lessons I learnt from the rooftops, caused me to get out of my own way, overcome my fears & jump into the unknown & make the decision to not go back to my career but instead.. make a massive difference & that's exactly what I did !

Was it scary? Of course, it was as it was the unknown & most definitely outside my comfort zone!
I mean I did not have a Business Degree & had no plan in site but what I did have was I could see the desired outcome and everyday I visualised it as already done! I saw myself delivering training to others & could truly see the gratitude from them as they truly understood & could therefore embrace and embed the training even more & therefore feel more empowered and confident should anything arise! I could see others sharing with how great the Training was & I could truly see the difference I was making and that is exactly what happened!

The Mind is so powerful & I really truly do understand that our thoughts lead to feelings lead to action and then results as that is exactly the formula I used! I dreamt it, felt it as done.. created Programs and action steps to make it happen and the testimonials that come in regularly as well as the International and National Business Awards affirm the results!

It is so funny as I even think back now and think.. Wow.. that is without any business plan in site but when your why is bigger than your why not, you become Unstoppable and that is exactly the formula I needed for how could I unknow this stuff? My incident happened for me and if I did not share from the rooftops, how could I live with myself knowing full well I was blessed to save our son, watch his milestones? This was way bigger than me & I had a responsibility to share the powerful lessons & when you come from a place of serving & place of making a difference & so clear on the desired outcome and see it as done.. the Universe conspires to MAKE IT HAPPEN.. another powerful lesson!

You see what I now realise is ...everything I needed was within me & my why became bigger than my why not as I suddenly had a message to deliver to help others realise I'm not unique & this can happen to anyone & what if they didn't have the skills I had?
How could I move past that guilt?

You see ... you can't un- know something once it happens especially for & not to you!

I felt chosen!

I now realise just how precious life is!

I became a crazy woman on a mission & suddenly as crazy as it sounds ...the training I created by sharing my experiences suddenly became highly sought after.... And that to me is CRAZY!! I still get goosebumps now to this day & know I am following my path!

Along with this, I am still so blessed to be involved in the media extensively, contribute to many books, co -author & contribute to many other Events, magazines, newspapers & national & International radio & podcast Shows ...

What a change!

I often sit back & think it's a dream & think just where I'd be & what I'd be doing right now, had God not have chosen me to make this difference! I realise now that nothing has meaning except the meaning you give & another person could have the same incident & have a totally different outcome or put a completely different meaning to the incident which is the gift! Others may still be victims and questioning why the incident occurred whereas I see the incident occurred because I asked for it and it most certainly has delivered many powerful lessons to get me into this space!

You see ... what I realise then is everything, every adversity I'd ever overcome to that point.. my crappy childhood.. EVERYTHING.. God was preparing me for that very moment as he knew I'd had the strength & resilience & the guts & determination to create something so many others would benefit & better protect their loved ones, but there's always more! Even my childhood were many gifts that were needed to help me on my path and dot to dot of this thing called Life! You see.. to me, I now realise life is constantly changing & now that Company, First Aid Yucan2 is set up & running effectively, leaving a legacy, isn't there others that had the same feeling or questioning, " is there more & perhaps, unfulfilled also?" How could I sit back, & know what I know & not do anything about it?

You see ... climbing a mountain is incredible but it's the lessons you learn along the way are POWERFUL! I knew then that others may not have the strength or mindset to overcome things like I was able...

GIFT! I have a responsibility to help others discover what I did, to be able to remove the clutter & tune into their heart space to discover their gifts, be reunited with their truths, life purpose but without the tragedy for if I don't step up & create.. How could I live with myself if others created similar tragedies? What if I could intervene and they learn what they need and discover their life purpose without the tragedy? Imagine how that would feel?

I do know & understand that with every tragedy, it's that person's journey & they learn many lessons as a result but what if they weren't as strong as I & they put a different meaning to the tragedy & even better.. what if they could discover what they needed, without the tragedy? I know I had the incident as I was chosen & it become a MUST to share, not a Should! I knew then I had a responsibility to create Programs, using different processes to help others remove blocks, fears so they can discover & then if they choose, shine their light brightly also! I had to stand up, show up, SHINE BRIGHTLY & be a Leader as the World needed me to!

Nothing lights me up more than when I witness the breakthroughs in my clients as I help them STOP limiting patterns that may have been there from childhood that have become patterns, to overcome any fears, to jump outside their comfort zone into the power zone, to truly understand that thing that happened, was a gift, to see it from another perspective so they too can stop listening to their head & tune into their heart as I did, to discover their gifts also & have the faith to follow the divine guidance we all have in our hearts , see, hear & feel the love all around & BE the change in the World they need to see!
Just something to be aware that our thoughts lead to feelings lead to action & results so what if you filled your life with positive thoughts & dreams & put the energy to those things and saw them as already done, rather than listening to the News & Naysayers…just what could YOU create?

What I have learnt through this journey by helping many others & being in the flow & having absolute clarity is that everything comes effortlessly with grace & ease when in this space & to be open to listening & seeing the synchronicities that show as a result! If we are stuck in our head that keeps us safe… we could quite easily miss those synchronicities and life can become difficult but investing the time to engage in Programs allows you to tune into your heart space where miracles truly do happen!

I am so grateful to have had the tragedies & attract the best people and resources into my life so I could truly understand & give me the reassurance I am most definitely on the right path & have a responsibility to share with others through Programs I have created! Nowadays I am so excited each and every day & feel my heart swell often and literally feel like Dorothy on the yellow brick road with her ruby red shoes with unlimited possibilities everywhere & open to hearing & making that impact & attracting many others that are aligned also. I love helping others have this realisation also to really show them anything is possible if you believe & put in the steps to make it happen.

It is of course a lot easier if you surround yourself with those that are likeminded and supportive which helps overcome any barriers or fears that come up.. We also run a Master class whereby we run weekly online sessions in a group environment, sharing the valuable tools we have learnt on our journey to carry out the inner work plus ways to protect you as you grow in an attempt to help others be reunited with their gifts and live their best lives yet!

The easiest way to create your own success is to mimic those who have already achieved.. It is great to have my Yucan2 Group to achieve this. Over this time I also was blessed to holistically regain my own health after 81/2 years of full-on treatments with 2 auto-immune diseases, where the prognosis was meant to be life long! It is so powerful to realise that mindset, along with a belief you can regain and sending energy to visualise and feel as if, along with many other things, that this is possible and is in fact another powerful tool that I am committed to share!

I now also love helping others regain or prevent ill health by being authentic & totally relatable & had a vision of creating an online Marketplace showcasing healthy, lifesaving & lifestyle products I could recommend, covering all things I am passionate about! Every day I could see it as done but had no idea how to create it but nor did I need to know either as by being so clear and sure it would happen, I manifested the right people to help me create and for my vision to become reality! Again, I do not share anything I have not carried out myself.. This stuff is so powerful and the reason I have gone through so much is to be able to share and help many others and bring them with me to reignite their lights so we can all live our best lives yet and make a big difference in this World so when our lives come to an end, we know we have achieved what we were meant to as life is so short and so precious & I know I am here to leave a legacy that will be remembered way after I leave and I am so excited to remind others & allow others to reignite their lights also! I felt like Noah with his Ark & didn't question but just continued to create & make my vision clearer! I've now partnered with an incredible friend who is also an expert in I T & Online Marketing, the two skills I needed to bring my vision into creation & I believe our paths were meant to cross.. another synchronicity!

Working with our strengths, we are most definitely in the flow & success is flowing in & even better ... we are able to serve even more, helping many others to do the same! During Covid, as the borders closed & I was no longer able to train & speak easily, I was forced to become resourceful & had to pivot & take all of my Training online so this was also the perfect time to launch our global Online Marketplace, as one of our Mentors suggested to give people what they want & with Covid still not in control, people are used to being at home & creatures of habit so will continue the online shopping they became accustomed to during the isolation & nowadays more than ever…are seeking healthy alternatives they could trust whilst giving them a chance to earn an income just by supporting, creating win/wins so here it is… Zenarah was launched!

We are never exempt from obstacles ourselves but have learnt to embrace & appreciate the obstacles & truly see the gifts as life is happening for us & share the lessons we learnt along this way! We certainly have the tools to continue to grow & understand we are bigger than any obstacle & can continue to overcome & learn more to share & help others & have a true understanding of being a light to many.

The more we overcome… the more we grow & come closer to our truth & really unveil more layers to reveal more so we can make even more of an impact & be the change in the World we need to see!

Our sons drowning most certainly happened for me to wake me up & tune into my heart space & has been a key to this & I'm so grateful for everything that has been created & the impact since that day!
I cannot wait to see just how much more of an impact I'll make by learning the big lessons from that day as well as what others achieve by learning all the lessons I learnt too!
Just keep dreaming & believing & working on yourself daily as anything is possible!

What lights me up, as I only share things I have found worked for us, is when clients receive their own positive results just by mimicking.
I am now known as the Manifesting Connections Queen as I remind others that our thoughts lead to feelings which lead to action and results so remind others via my stories to be mindful of our thoughts as we can not only create good things, but full on things also.. Using this philosophy I am relatable and live my life this way & share what I have personally learnt so walk the talk.. Since.. created multiple businesses for solutions for today's big problems & I love helping others, through being relatable and vulnerable to share my tools I learnt so they can tune into this energy, be reignited & reunited with their truths & their gifts so they can live a more fulfilled happy life!
What I do know is we are all different & it's those differences that make us unique & it's coming together with others that have different gifts to truly rise & make a big difference in this World.
With my Business partner, and I it is our strengths and identifying them & working with them that truly compliments what we do & allows us to progress & make a big difference in this World effortlessly with grace & ease!

You see, we cannot be the expert in everything, but if we do know what lights us up and what our strengths are.. we can then ask for what we need to fulfil the roles we are not so great at & remember to listen and watch for the synchronicities as we ask.. Clarity breeds power & when we are clear of what we need, the Universe most certainly delivers! As we grow and evolve & live in our truth & power whilst shining our light brightly, we can absolutely be vulnerable of jealous people so it is so important & I have learnt through my own experiences, to protect ourselves daily as not everyone has the same good intent as you!

Working on yourself daily, doing the inner work is an essential part of your growth & in particular, protecting yourself.. You cannot un know experiences!
I share some of the Stories in a closed environment which is safe, with the idea to be vulnerable & share just what has happened and just what has shown up to protect me as a result!

It is crazy to think that others can project & inflict this hurt on others due to jealously especially when they do not know or understand just what that person has been through in their life & the lessons they have learnt & the work they have carried out in their personal time to create the success, but unfortunately.. it does exist especially when you are a light impacting the World in a positive way so it is an essential thing to learn.

Not only is it important to learn from those that have been through it in an attempt to accelerate your own success but by being relatable and sharing, it is a real reminder how our thoughts create our reality so it is important to remember this! By being immersed in a Community, it allows a forum to share, be accountable, lift each other up on the tough days whilst celebrating wins along the way! Remember that who you surround yourself with, you become!

Our Yucan2 Community is designed to help you discover your "Y", by deciding Yucan so YUCAN live a life your Deserve!
I myself have also been blessed to overcome many years of ill health where the prognosis was not good as well as many tragedies by using the tips and tools I share! These tools are essential to have in your toolkit to create success and fulfilment!

Life is constantly preparing you for what's to come & I see this now in my own life, just like a dot to dot, but if you do not capture this, it could be totally missed! We've been prepared for sure & ready & open for incredible things to come! It's so amazing to have the faith that we are always protected no matter what gets thrown our way!

Have faith to follow the divine guidance in our hearts & help many others to always see the beauty in every situation to truly understand things are constantly happening for and not to you & see the unlimited possibilities as a result.. By being relatable & vulnerable to share, believe this allows others to stay committed to their own cause & believe that the best Coaches are those that have been through their own personal experiences so they can get out of their head & into their heart!

Tammy Ritchie

Find out more about Tammy at <u>www.firstaidyucan2.com.au</u>
<u>www.yucan2.com.au</u>
<u>www.zenarah.com</u>

<u>Facebook:</u>
<u>https://www.facebook.com/tammy.richie</u>
<u>https://www.facebook.com/zenarahmarketplace/</u>
<u>https://www.facebook.com/yucan2/</u>
<u>https://www.facebook.com/FirstAidYUCAN2/</u>

<u>Linked In:</u>
<u>https://www.linkedin.com/in/tammyrichie1972/</u>

<u>Twitter:</u>
<u>https://twitter.com/firstaidtammy</u>

<u>Instagram:</u>
<u>https://www.instagram.com/tammy.richie/</u>

IN THE QUIET MOMENTS

One of the things that gave me much pleasure reading were the pieces where friends shared their inner thoughts. Of course, clinically, this is always of interest to me, but the bravery to share with the world, those thoughts in the quiet moments was just amazing.

When we are still, when we are quiet, our inner thoughts can creep up and the most negative of those thoughts seem to clunk around with the heaviest of footsteps. *"I will fail at the job interview." "I will never meet anyone who can love me." "I have no friends." "I can't do it." "I will never achieve anything."*

In the cognitive behavioural therapy world, these are called negative belief systems and these little suckers can be difficult to turn around. Not impossible of course with the right techniques but truly difficult to change. This is because most of these beliefs, these inner thoughts have taken a lifetime to grow in strength and determination. We learn most of our values and our thoughts about ourselves and the world around us, when we are children. Of course, these negative beliefs left unchecked take on a whole life of their own. So, that by the time, I have a client sitting in front of me, they may have been inadvertently feeding these negative belief systems for a good forty years or more. We are not going to change these permanently in our first sixty-minute session together.

Working with psychologists and counsellors for years, I remember in one workplace a psychologist friend made us all complete the schema questionnaires. These are a series of several hundred very short questions that you must answer with the first answer that fits. Based on the scoring, you are then assigned a number of schemas that are prevalent in your thinking. I remember one person coming back with nothing to report. Her scores suggested there were no underlying schemas attached to their decision making. The psychologist was outraged. How could this be? He demanded she go back and redo the questionnaire. She must have lied in her answers.

The results came back the same and when we were asked to repeat the questionnaire a couple of years later, her responses were no different. This was a woman who basically had her stuff worked out. She was conscious in her decision making, recognising the way she wanted to live and lived everyday according to those self-imposed values.

Never before nor after this incident have I seen scores like hers. All of the rest of us, as educated and worldly as we believed ourselves to be, had some underlying schemas that weren't helpful to our thinking and decision making. The great thing is that mine had changed. From the first questionnaire to the next one two years later, my scores had changed, partly a conscious decision to make the change but also, I am sure through unconscious decision making based on this newly found self-identification.

The very first step in making any change is to first identify and acknowledge the change to be made. One friend wrote along the lines of... even if you can't admit something to someone else, find the courage to admit it to yourself first. Here, we go, more free therapy. Hope you are still enjoying it.

I found such admiration for the writers who shared some of their thoughts in the quieter moments. Hope you are inspired as well.

Kellie M Cox

Happiness is the opposite of sadness. The two are like order and chaos, the yin and yang of our psyche, perfectly balanced, one cannot exist without the other. Therefore, when we strive for happiness, we must accept that if we are successful, we will be equally as sad. Instead of happiness, strive to be content. To put your head on your pillow each night and say to yourself "I have done enough." The belief that not only is it all going to be okay in the end but that it is okay right now.

Connor Renwick

The noise and the nose...

Have you ever noticed that in calm moments, you can bring yourself to hear just the quietest noise or smell a slight fragrance in the air? You might in those moments strain to hear, or follow the scent...

We can't help but find ourselves in a whirl at times...work, deadlines, dramas, noisy interiors, buzzing outdoors. In the moments when we have to think, we almost can't – stop your brain may say – stop I can't think!

Sometimes that whir, that noise, that overload comes to feel overwhelming...obscuring not just your senses but also your sense.

My best advice has come to me from the depths of grief, from the tensest anxiety and from the grip of paralysing fear...it is this...

No matter what is going on around you, you have two sure things:

The first is the power to bring your attention, your inner narrator and your senses into the very present, and if in the very present you are not unsafe; you have time to come into the moment and take only one small step and move ever so slightly.

The second is the secure knowledge that the sun will set, and the days will collect, and you will come to other moments, and some of those will be in peace.

In your days, ahead of the grief we know we have to experience, ahead of the struggle work or relationships or life will bring, and before the unexpected, take the time to practice turning down the noise, follow your nose, bring your senses to your survival, your peace. The calm you find will carry, carry your calm.

Karen Cutler, Lawyer, Sport Photographer and Trivia Host.

Ask

One general advice that I would offer to others as well as to myself is to find out what one wants truly at that moment in time and ask for it or express it. We are sure to get it.

"Ask and you shall receive" yes, it sounds conservative, religious and it is so biblical and I claim to come from an alternative way of thinking[!!!], but this statement for whatever it means is so true if only one has that strength to know what one wants and ask for it.   To arrive at what we genuinely want is something most of us struggle. Why do we struggle? Back during the days when I worked as a residential educator and taking care of a bunch of 18 bubbling teenaged girls, they would often come to me to check about what dress to wear, what accessories would go with their dress or what subjects to study that day or what chores to do...the list was endless...initially I took time to sit with them and deliberated, spent few hours and came up with my decision and would let them know. To my surprise they would choose exactly the opposite of what I chose and give me reasons as to why they feel otherwise. To save my time [and also to avoid my disappointments !!!] I kept small papers in my room and when they came to me, I would quickly write their choices in two small chits of papers and fold it and ask them to select it for themselves. But before they did it, I asked them to close their eyes and think for that moment as to what they would really like that paper they pick need to have, most of the times they knew exactly what they want and they would just go back with a smile even without picking up the paper. This whole process of expressing what one truly wants, yet struggling to express the same set me thinking. Then it dawned on me, that these girls of mine actually knew what they wanted but had trouble expressing it for want of an external validation, simple acknowledgement of their choices. I then realised, it's not just these teenaged girls, it's also us... how much we are trained to depend on others to validate what we want rather, just say what we want irrespective of what others think.

I believe that we all know what we want yet we do not say it aloud for the fear of being ridiculed by others, fear of being shamed when others know what one really wants, and what image it would create of them in others' mind, also our moral compass and deep-rooted conditioning of our past does not allow us to acknowledge it and express it. We also want others to say 'yes' to what we think we want and so on. Being a counsellor I was trained to elicit from the clients, what they really want out of the session. It is also one of the main skills that we got trained to ask, "What is that single most important thing they want?". Once it is elicited it is understood the path towards it is fairly easy. Saying this I would also add that we need to be careful what we ask for, for when we get it there is no way of turning away from its consequences. Sometimes I think we do not ask what we want is because of this very reason, "consequence" we want something, but we do not want to face the consequences which would come along.

If only, we take a moment to sit with ourselves, close our eyes like what I did with my girls, and figure out what we 'truly' want of that moment, say it aloud and not be bothered about what others think of it because that is what we really want and we will have the courage to stand by it, as we have found out what we truly want. And once we have figured out what we truly want, we need to ask or express it because we will surely get it.
Ending it with a little humour about the warning I gave…

A woman put an ad that said, "Looking for a husband"
The next day she received hundreds of letters that said: Can you take mine?"

Karpagam Subramani, Counsellor, 46 years young.

Bathe regularly and eat well.

Tyson

She pulls him closer to her using powers of persuasion from the deepest depths of her being.

The sexy siren that is his mermaid dances with the awakened man.

His mythical muse skims lightly over the white dunes bringing him closer to her.

She entices him to her shores to flirt with his senses.

He is powerless to her call.

Her warm salt air kisses his mouth lightly as he licks the magic potion from his lips.

His heart pounds to the sounds of the rhythmical motion of her crashing waves as he is drawn closer.

He watches as the flowing blonde locks of the goddess from the sea, delves once more deeply into the water and he knows he must follow.

He smells the scent of the ocean, his mistress once more, the purity of the sea overwhelms his senses.

The white foam from the top of the wave daringly brushes past his thigh, tantalising the skin, bringing a warmth he had craved.

And with one final act of courage, he too disappears beneath the surface of her liquid embrace.

And in that moment, he is finally free, his soul, it has been cleansed.

Kellie M Cox

Happiness, Abundance and Unconditional Love

Happiness

Happiness is innate. It is very personal.

Nearly everyone has a different idea about what is happiness. Some may overlap slightly or greatly – such as the feeling you get when a child achieves or learns something they have never done or known before – and others come from a completely different place – such as why some people are passionate about a certain football team or code, and other absolutely hate them with an almost equal and opposite energy.

Happiness is layered.

At the superficial, or shallowest, level, happiness can come and go quickly and be lost in an instant of time. For example, you buy a brand new car and take it for a drive. You feel happy and delight in all the newness of it: the smell, the colour, the dash, the buttons, the features, the sound system! Everything is brilliant and it's yours in this moment. You drive a few kilometres and approach a roundabout. Applying the brakes is a little strange, but they work efficiently. Your head is still in this bubble of bliss. Suddenly someone rushes through without slowing and you panic a little – DON'T TOUCH MY CAR! They stop and miss you, but at that moment, your palms are sweaty, your heart is racing and your mouth is yelling obscenities at this moron! Your happiness has vanished instantly.

A deeper level of happiness can be felt when you connect with other people at an emotional or intellectual level. You have similar values and beliefs, and you can relax in each other's company. You can be more yourself and not feel like you need to put on a certain persona to be accepted. You don't have to 'buy' your way into the group to belong; just be yourself.

As time moves forward and your experiences are both good and bad, and sometimes tragic, you realise that real happiness doesn't come from the things you can possess or with whom you spend your time. When you lose a very close friend or family member, the sense of loss is so deep and egregious that the grief threatens to engulf you. Denial and bargaining don't work or help; nothing can change the fact that the loss is real and feels so final. Time cannot be reversed and actions undone. Regrets cannot be appeased.

The lesson to learn is total acceptance.

Accept that things change in life and you have little or no influence on them. You certainly can't control them. You can only control what you think, so it's important to be balanced in your thoughts. This can come from a deep sense of gratitude for everything you have and from what you have experienced in your life. Humility comes from an awareness of the lessons all around you. Recognising that you do not know everything, and that there is something to be learned on a daily basis, sometimes from the most unlikely incidents or simple people, is very humbling.

Abundance

Developing a sense of abundance is easy. Recognise what you need on a daily basis in all aspects of your life and that is enough. When you have enough, you have abundance; no more, no less.

Unconditional Love

The wagging tail of a dog or the purr of a cat is unconditional love. They are happy and content to see you and be with you as you are, in this moment. No strings attached. Just you as you are and them as they are.

To express unconditional love for another is one of the deepest and purest emotions we can feel and show to another. You might think you will become vulnerable to open yourself up like this, but in fact, the opposite is true because they will feel your openness and feel safe in your presence; safe enough to reciprocate in kind and open up to you.

The love a parent feels when they hold their new-born child for the first time is an expression of this type of love. Wonder intermingled with an intense sense of protection and responsibility; this incredibly vulnerable baby is relying on you to nurture, guide, and care for them until they are strong and capable enough to thrive on their own. That is the responsibility of a parent and the rewards are there to enjoy on a daily basis. The petty little things are just that, so they should be given a moment to learn the lesson hidden within, and then released.

No baggage.

When you let go of all the insignificant things that hold you back, it's like dropping a huge 45kg backpack. You stand straighter, you feel lighter, and you interact with your loved ones with renewed vigour and honesty. If they have done bad things to you, forgive them unreservedly and tell them so. Ask them for their forgiveness for all the bad things you have done to them, even if you can't remember what they might have been. Don't recall the experiences – you don't want to relive them – just release them and don't look back.

Move forward in your life with those things that are important to you.

Stay honest and integrous and be compassionate to all things around you.

This brings you contentment and true happiness, because you know nothing can take these feelings and 'knowings' from you. They cannot be lost. Your contentment is real and safe.

Kerri Yarsley, Writer/Editor, age 63.

If you can't admit to others, then find the courage to admit to yourself when you're not ok. The heaviness will lift you and you will see tomorrow.

On a slightly less darker note, learn to laugh at yourself, it's bloody terrific.

Rebecca Mander, Organic Cosmetologist, @cos.organicsau.

WHEN PEOPLE DISSAPOINT... BECAUSE IT WILL HAPPEN

Look, let's be realistic for a moment, some people suck. My best friend and I have a saying around this, which I can't share here, but many of you have heard it. It's not that all or even most people are sucky, it is just helpful to remember that some people are sent to test us.

The enormous benefit of this, is the great learning we get from these experiences. The experiences are what make us who we become. One of the contributors shared this very thought. It is not to just to remember the good times but to learn from every experience.

People often ask me if I have any regrets and you know besides not thinking to buy up more Gold Coast property prior to the Covid pandemic, probably not. But really, who would have guessed that every southerner who could, would move to the Gold Coast when they went into lockdown in their states.

Looking back, there is really nothing that I could have done differently, ok marriage number two was a bit of a waste of time and money, but when married I did adopt my beautiful German Shepherd girl, Rose Jasmine Petal. So, something good did come out of those years.

I married for the first time, very young. I was 21 years old when I stood outside my family home in my wedding dress, my bouquet in hand waiting for the rest of the family to pull the car around, so we could get to the church. I remember very clearly standing there and thinking, *if just one of my friends, anyone of them came screeching into the quiet cul de sac, threw open the car door and yelled "get in!" I would have.* But fortunately, none of them did and I went on to say "I do" that very day, and only a short few years later my two beautiful sons were born. I started my family quite early; I was 23 and 25 when my two boys were born.

I became a single mother at 25, not through any choice of my own. The rigors of work and family life don't suit everyone, and the calls of secret affairs and late-night parting were more appealing to my husband's lifestyle. So, at a very young age, I was single again, working full time, raising two babies under two and studying a Bachelor of Science, majoring in psychology. There is not a single thing I would change about any of that. Now approaching fifty years of age, I am surrounded by loving adult children. I acquired another along the way in the form of a stepdaughter, who is like a daughter to me. As their partners join the family and I hope one day for grandchildren, I can honestly look back and say that everything happened just as it was meant to.

Life wasn't by any means easy, I lost all ability to sleep somewhere in there, but I gained not only a gorgeous family but a long lasting and successful career in psychology and counselling that has spanned over two decades already.

A chapter on sucky people, really isn't complete without a

reference to the white witch. I worked for quite a number of years in a workplace that I loved until one day, the white witch was employed and for some reason, just despised my friends and me. I was like poison in the workplace for her. If anyone was seen talking to me, she instantly wanted them fired. So as punishment for my existence in her workplace, this manager placed me in a tiny corner office next to the photocopier and then threw in another person she equally despised to join my team.

This broom cupboard of an office was so small that if I wanted to use the bathroom, I had to ask my colleague to push his chair in so I could get past. If I took even a day's annual leave, my colleague would re-arrange the furniture to try to find a way for us each to co-exist. One particular configuration meant I had to climb under my desk to get to the bathroom. We were either going to fall madly in love or kill each other. There really were no other options for two people having to spend hours every day forced together in such a small space.

Well as it turned out, he fell in love with me (he will deny this) and me with him. I consider him one of the most important people in my life. We both have a little PTSD from the years of working together. We message each other most days, sometimes I think because we just got so used to being in each other's faces that we have to keep the conversation flowing. But beyond that, I absolutely love him to bits, and I talk about him to everyone all the time.

The funny thing about the white witch who thought that throwing us together into this tiny, little room would force us to quit is that we have forgotten her real name. You know, on the odd occasion that we remember her, neither of us can remember her actual name. It might take a while, then one of us will remember. But for this person, so full of her own importance, thinking that she would be able to ruin our lives, we don't even remember her. But you know what, the best friend that she gifted me, he will be in my life forever.

Another great gift this experience gave me was my epic travel experiences. As I had long service leave and was clearly not wanted in the workplace, I bought a one way ticked to Rome with two months up my sleeve to travel through Europe and that experience for me was life changing. I returned to work with the firm decision I would quit. I had to give a month's notice which would make my last day the 1st April. It happened to be the same day, my house sale was coming through, so I thought all the stars were aligned. I came to work and by best friend (who didn't want me to leave) talked me into not resigning on the very first day back. The second morning when I came to work, the white witch called me into a meeting.

She had bad news for me, she shared through a smirk. My position was being made redundant. I was to finish in my role on the 1st April. Of course, they would love me to move to another department, but if not the offer of redundancy was on the table. It took all my effort not to smile. Twenty-four hours earlier and I would have resigned, but here they were offering me a tidy little sum of money to finish up. "You must be sad," white witch offered."

"Yes," I lied, my acting has never been good, but it was enough to get me through.

"You should go home now then and start looking for other

work. No need to work out the notice period. We will pay that all out to you."

Woohoo! I jumped into the car and came and stayed on the coast. For the entire month of March, I am pretty sure I was the highest paid beach bum on the coast. Days were all about catching the sun and swimming in the ocean.

So, the morale of the story is…some people will suck. Some people will walk into your life and throw it into disarray…and that's ok. When it happens, and it will…take a deep breath, look straight at the situation in front of you and ask yourself, what is this person here to teach me.

Then, learn the lesson quickly and slam that door shut right in their face. Walk away, shoulders high, chest out and own whatever that experience has taught you.

And the closing the door analogy is of equal importance here because, as the saying goes, when one door closes, another opens. And who knows what great joy and wonder will surprise us behind the very next door.

Kellie M Cox

Chances are that those who profess to be there
unconditionally will serve their own
needs and be angry, upset and manipulate you for making you feel
responsible for
their own horrendous behaviours.

So, live to be open - to recognise those wonderful souls who are so
rare and are so beautiful and who celebrate unending notions of your
true self.

Phoenix Sparkles

People often say, "focus on the good times" when referring to a challenging break-up or end of a relationship however stop and think 'what new skill, thought pattern or experience did I leave with'. Every relationship that crosses our paths has something to teach us and adds to our personal growth however it is not always easy to see.

Portia, OT, age 30.

The land-dwelling mortal
With the dark brooding eyes
Half man
Half child

Whimsical with his affection
He fears persecution
Delusion of grandeur torment his mind

Unable to feel
Without a conscious
His black heart feeds on those who believe

Truth…the only redemption for the mortal with a soul

Kellie M Cox

Invest yourself in the right people

Sheena Yso

Poseidon lowered his trident tearing at the flesh of the mythical creature.

Releasing in an instant the baited hook of humanity's evil wedged deep in her soul.

Glistening in the sun's rays her scales magically heal the wound, covering the bloodied mess with sparkling sequins, her treasures from the sea.

The mermaid looked toward the ocean, her heart softening once more.

She bid farewell to the hard earth beneath her and leapt to the depths of her home for she no longer felt fear.

Her mind awakened as the last of her mortal remains were lost to the tide, she watched as her broken persona slip away into the dark waters.

Never again was she to return to the cruel land, for she was now free.

Kellie M Cox

"Love all; Trust a few; Do wrong to none".

It's from **All's Well That Ends Well.**

It's my favourite quote and my general guideline for interpersonal relationships. Especially "trust a few" because when you trust people on the face value, they sometimes just betray your trust and let you down.

Patrick Ryan, Filmmaker, age 41.

FINDING BEAUTY

Have you ever been around someone, who just stops mid-sentence to say, "Look at the colours in that sky." These people are my favourite people to be around. I remember driving my kids crazy with these moments when they were young. I would stop and strongly encourage them to stop too and look at the colours in the sky, the fragrance of a flower, the majesty of the ocean. They whined every time, which just made me do it even more.

Beauty is not just found in the things around us in nature, but in music, in food, in people's laughter. It could be the most single underrated virtue in the world. Finding beauty for me is very closely aligned to making memories. I vividly remember places I have visited and things I have experienced. I remember when I was younger, I must have been twelve, although I swear I was much older as I remember being in Hawaii to celebrate my big sister's twenty-first birthday and arguing with my mother because she wouldn't let me go with my big sister to a party with the locals. Sorry mum! But on this trip, I remember stopping into a little pit stop and enjoying a thick piece of cheese on a warm slice of freshly baked bread. The taste was so divine, I have tried to emulate it ever since. Similarly, I remember this little cake shop underneath our hotel in Hong Kong and after a day shopping with the parents, my little sister and I would go in and get a piece of chocolate cake to take back up the room. I still remember every delicious morsel.

On a much more recent trip, I spent hours taking photos inside the empty Palais Garnier or the Place de I' Opera in Paris. Inside the theatre is the chandelier that featured in the story of The Phantom of the Opera. I swear it is impossible to look away, it is simply so exquisite. I am sure anyone watching on thought I was a crazy as I stood beside the red velvet opera chairs running my hand over the velvet, first one way and then another as I imagined all the people who had stood there before me enjoying the immense beauty of this exquisite room.

Recently I was enjoying an author talk of one of the best-selling Australian authors of all time. The talk was of course over champagne brunch in a little French restaurant. The author spoke of attending the opera in Paris and the feel of the red velvet chair beneath her hand. I swear I had tears, actually tears in my eyes as her description brought back to me every sensation of being in that very same opera house. I cannot wait to email her and tell her exactly that. On second thoughts… I better not scare her off before she gets to know me a bit better.

Beauty to me equates to memories. Those moments of stopping, and of using every sense of touch, taste, smell, sight and sound, these are the moments that appear to embed into our memories forever. I have shared in this chapter, my blog from my travel to Rome. This city and its people force the traveller to stop and appreciate the beauty. People not only admire the beauty of their historical city but go about creating new beauty each day through their music, their food, their limoncello, that they encourage you to try over and over again. I hope you enjoy stopping for a bit and enjoying the beauty my friends have written about. And I hope you are inspired to stop each day and find the beauty around you.

Kellie M Cox

Blog - I lost my heart in Rome…

Travelling through Italy has been the most beautiful experience and I choose that word purposefully. Everything in Rome is beautiful; everyone I have met in this ancient city is beautiful. And it is the people most of all that contribute to this beauty. Unlike, traditional western cultures, the Italians and particularly the Romans have no interest in what you do for work. They appear to care little about how busy your career is or how you meet your key performance indicators for the month. This is a sweeping generalisation of course and I am sure there would be those in business in Rome that would enjoy eliciting those conversations with you, but for those working and living in the ancient district of Rome, those working with the tourism machine that perpetuates the hive of activity in the city, those individuals want to know about you, the person. It is a great relief to not be asked immediately, what you do for work, but instead asked about who your family is, where you are from and what you love. These seem to be the central three questions afforded to a new acquaintance in Rome and once these parameters or criteria are addressed, a new friendship is formed. It really appears to be that easy.

It seems to me similar to primary or nursery school where friendships are formed instantly based on mutual love. Two young girls enjoy the same music, and they are bonded. Young boys, bond on the football field and become lifelong friends. The complexity of modern society is forgotten or rejected, whichever may be the case in this city of beauty. And once those parameters are determined and the friendship is formed, the two new acquaintances go about the business of enjoying the beauty together.

And for those of you with an idea of what that means, yes, this beauty can absolutely be found in the desire of the flesh, but this is one and only one avenue for the exploration of beauty. Beauty is found in every corner of this impressive city. It is found in every narrow alley and in every cobblestoned piazza. Beauty is present in every movement, sound, touch and feel that tantalises the senses. Your new Roman friend will seek out with you, beautiful food, music, wine or as the locals prefer, Limoncello, the Italian made lemon liquor they will so fondly serve you and insist you enjoy. In some cases, the enjoyment of Limoncello is a long and entertaining process that can last many hours, long into the night as if each new tasting will be miraculously different to the last.

It would appear to this wide-eyed traveller that exploring beauty in Rome is the city's most treasured pastime. Well-known musicians take to the streets to play for the crowds, asking nothing but the purity of enjoyment and appreciation of the romantic sounds being created. Dining out is a gastronomic feast with every pasta and pizza imaginable being offered up as fare for the hungry tourist and local alike. The most passionate of the foodies offering just a little chilli or just a little special garlic sauce, fresh parmesan or locally made pure virgin olive oil to tantalise the senses even further. There is no point in declining the helpful suggestions; these artists know just what to add to turn the meal from food into an explosion of the taste buds.

Artwork, statues and ornate facades of buildings burst from every pore of the mighty ancient city. Influences from Egypt, massive pillars and obelisks create a sense of majesty and greatness. The beauty of the city itself challenges the traveller and dares one not to fall in love. The archeological lasagna as it is called is the result of centuries of building a city torn down time and time again by the ravages of war and years. The hidden treasures beneath old churches and museums, incomprehensible from the outside, supply miles of ancient ruins that will take your breath away. The imaginations of city life centuries before, forces the witness to testify to the rich history of this glorious city.

Beauty is not forced but adored in this busy place. A city never too rushed to stop and appreciate its uniqueness. For a traveller, a willing participant on the search, you will see, taste, hear, touch and feel beauty in every form. You will be appreciated yourself for the beauty of your soul. A lovely and very professional taxi driver showed me some of the local highlights, including a real-life centurion as he toured me across Rome one night. He waited until I had stepped from the vehicle to tell me I was beautiful. "I had to wait until you were out of the taxi to tell you how beautiful you are. You are very, very beautiful." He had obviously not wanted me to feel uncomfortable or threatened in any way. I swear the tears welled in my eyes. The strong, independent woman in me wanted to roar to herself for needing to have a complete stranger make her feel beautiful again. But this man, this Roman-born taxi driver wanted to appreciate and announce the beauty he saw. I could feel nothing but honoured by his compliment.

I will travel through Europe, meeting beautiful people and visiting beautiful places but for the challenge to seek beauty in everything I will never find anywhere like Rome.

A little bit of me, of my interaction with people will hopefully stay with those I meet along my journey, but forever and always a little bit of my heart will have been lost to Rome.

Kellie M Cox

She giggles

She laughs
She flutters right past

Not a care in the world
Or a thought on her mind

Her smile is bright
Eyes are a-light

And her words of wisdom brought this adult insight.

If you don't want to go, don't go

Life is your choice, make them for you.

Happy is an emotion
Emotions are fleeting
Contentment a goal
That's worth achieving

The only person you'll live with your whole life is you
So do the best things for you that you can do.

Delilah

Advice for life!

Life - something I strongly believe is underrated, constantly complained about & often taken for granted. "Enjoy" sounds simple, & for a lot of people it isn't quite that simple – but I believe there is joy and enjoyment in so much of our lives that goes unnoticed.

My advice? Notice them! The beautiful day, your hot shower, your cosy bed, the ability to go about your daily life with relative ease. The seasons, tasting your favourite food & your friendships, family, pets... the list goes on and on.

Now, that you have been blessed with the gift of arriving at 50, even more reason to enjoy life!

You will also know/should know by now, that you will not find enjoyment in material items that clutter up our homes and offer a short lived 'buzz' upon purchasing – quickly to be put down and forgotten about or jammed into the back of an already full wardrobe to collect dust – no. You will find joy in the faces of your loved ones, your children, voices of your friends, the familiar smell of your most treasured places that cement into your mind forever, just sharing your time is truly the greatest gift of all!

So, my dear friend-enjoy this time you have been gifted, smell, see, listen, travel, taste, eat, drink & be merry – and enjoy 50 & beyond!

Catherine, working mother of two, age 36.

Life is precious. Life is short. Don't take it for granted

Never underestimate the positive potential of even small actions

Know the value of your contribution

To love and be loved; that is a blessed life

At the end of the day, take the time to reflect, identify and name three great things about your day. Sometimes you need to find small things, and that's ok.

Usha

FAMILY... WHATEVER THAT LOOKS LIKE

Family takes many forms. There is of course the family you are born into, the family that you choose and the family you create. I have a wonderful group of chosen sisters. One I have known for thirty-five years and the others for more than twenty years. Wow, I am old! I won't name names and hence divulge ages. Don't worry girls!

I was recently introduced to a friend's sister and she introduced me as her chosen sister. I joked that by that title, we too must now be chosen sisters and she replied with the most delightful of notions. She said, "All women are sisters."

Many clients I see, bring to their sessions hurt from their family of origin, both historical and current. Some writers here, have shared their own stories of family and the hardships as well as the joys that family have created. I use an exercise in counselling sessions, involving a series of circles each one extending out around the one before. I ask my clients to consider each circle as a different band or level of friendship/family. They are to place the names of the people in their lives within these circles.

The first circle the smallest one is themselves. The individual person is after all the most significant. The relationship with yourself is the most critical and important one you will ever have. In the next smallest circle. I ask my client to write down the names of the people who would die for them. Or if we are being slightly less dramatic, the first people they would ring if something went wrong. These are the people that would drop everything and say, "I'm on my way!" The next circle are close friends or family – people who they feel good being around, people who offer invites to events; the people that remember the special events and do a check in every so often.

The next circle are the names of the people who are maybe bordering on this close friendship, but not quite there yet, they might be new people or people who come and go from their lives. They may be people who they would like to get to spend more time with, people they share common values and goals with.

The next larger circle are what I would call acquaintances, people they may work with, but are not very close to; people who they can enjoy a conversation with but they probably wouldn't invite over to their house for coffee. These could also be people who are transitioning into the inner circles as they get to spend more time with them and get to know and trust them better.

On the outside of the last and largest circle are the people whom for whatever reason are a part of their life occasionally or through family but not really people they trust or spend time with. They might see them occasionally at a family event. They might see them at university or school, but they don't actively want to engage with them in their lives. These can also be the people who have hurt the client; people who have to remain in their lives for a specific reason but who have proven their inability to be trusted. One client called these people her toxic people.

What is important with this exercise is that it is constantly evolving. People are moving inwards and outwards through the circles. New relationships are formed and as trust is built these people move inwards into those close circles of friend and family.

After they have the names in the correct circles, they then assign a measure to each circle. This measure can be a single number or a percentage and this number represents the amount of time and energy they focus on this group of family and friends. It goes back to the widely viewed ideal that – what you nurture grows. The more time you spend on something, the more that thing develops as a result of the attention of your love and energy. What many clients find in this aspect of the exercise, is that they are spending much more time and energy concerned about the toxic people, those people on the outside of the circle. They often find that acquaintances and colleagues received more time than the people in their inner most circle – the people who would die for them. One client had just one person in her inner circle, her mother, the person she said would die for her and would do anything for her anytime she needed it, but she reflected that she hadn't even returned her mother's phone call for weeks.

She was too busy worrying about the toxic people, that she had neglected the relationship that meant the most to her in the world. The final step is to re-align those numbers, put down a goal number or percentage of time they want to spend in each area of their lives. That might mean for some clients, re-arranging their free time, ensuring that they drop in on friends or at the very least a phone call or message to say hi.

The next session, we evaluate how they have gone. How did

they spend the preceding week? Where was their energy and time spent? Was it worrying about the toxic people or getting bogged down with the outside circles or was it where they wanted to spend time on nurturing existing close relationships and potentially directing some energy into forming closer ties with people that they shared similar values and goals to? I have found this to be a powerful exercise and my clients love it. They always go home and during the week add people to the circles and move people around. The change in one week for some clients has been dramatic. They return with a lightness about them, a contentment and happiness.

It is because the energy they put out is also the energy they get back and when they focused their intent and time on the right people, they received far more back in return. It is a simple realignment of time and energy.

And of course, in the following sessions, once the person is re-energised, we can start to work on that all important inner circle, the circle with their name in it. This is the most important work of all.

I personally do a similar thing on my phone. I often look at my messages to see who I have as my top five most recent contacts. This is not to say that everyone I message isn't important, they certainly are, but I do get requests daily from people near and far and I can get quite behind on returning back messages. I wish I was better but there are only so many hours in a day. So, every so often I make sure I check my phone to make sure my family and my closest friends are in that top 5.

My kids quite often are, but if they have slipped below that line, I might even just send them a funny meme (well.. I always find them funny, they don't always), or a photo of the dogs, or the garden or pool. I do this because although I know they are busy and won't have time to message, I want them to know I am thinking of them. I do wish they would reply with the laughing emoji on the memes, but well that just encourages me to find better memes next time.

I am mindful of this also when I come out of a busy day of client work, or student assessments, where I haven't even been able to check my phone, let alone reply to messages. I can and often do have many messages and missed calls to respond to. At the first chance, and this is normally when I hop in the car to leave work, I do a quick scan to look for the kids names and they always, always get the first call back. I know everyone had something important to contact me about, but my energy and time goes first and foremost to my inner circle.

My chosen sisters and close friends are always a close second and that is because as the title of this chapter suggests - family is whatever you want that to look like. I never knew three of my grandparents. They had all died before I was born. My nana, who I loved very much died when I was in my twenties, my father passed when I was in my thirties and since then it really has just been my mum left. I don't see much of my biological family, the odd Christmas or birthday dinner when we get together. So, I created my own family, through birth; through people who I love who became my children and with friends who became my sisters. And of course, I can't forget the fur babies, who made themselves an integral part of our family from the moment they stepped their tiny little paws into our home.

I know through my client work that family can provide so much joy but also so much anxiety. And for those people without family, it can be lonely. So, my advice is family is whatever you make it. You create your own family. Hopefully the stories shared in this chapter will create some joy and inspiration around what family looks like.

Kellie M Cox

When your kids are wanting your time and attention; when they wake you in the night because they need your comfort; when they wake you too early because they want to be with you; when they don't even let you shower or go to the toilet alone…ENJOY IT!

In the blink of an eye, they will be gone and will turn to others to get their needs met, and will have a life of their own that you will only get a small share of - a minor part in. Life goes by really fast, savour those precious moments when you get to be the whole world to another person.

Deb, age 70.

I was very fortunate growing up in that I had parents who not only advocated the importance of caring and service for others but lived this important guideline for living a meaningful life. My parents and grandparents sponsored refugees to Australia after WW2, so early on, my brother and I learned through our relationships with people from war torn countries, what a gift this was to us, enriching our lives. That was well over 70 years ago, and since then I am so grateful for the many opportunities that have presented themselves for reaching out to others, from working at the age of 16 with leukaemia patients, to working with refugees from Ethiopia in Sudan in the '80s and now with many friends in Myanmar/ Burma. However, this all starts in our families, and is extended through our relationships with our friends, where we learn and practice giving and receiving love. It's love that 'makes the world go around,' some song says. Some years ago, I spent a weekend with Uncle Max - a Yuin Elder, at Mt Gulaga sacred site near Tilba, and we could see his love and respect for ALL of life, even after the massacres his people had suffered earlier on. Our loving relationships start in our families and we share this with others. I feel so blessed to have three beautiful daughters, a loving extended family and families who have adopted me into theirs from Myanmar and India. Of course, life has its ups and downs, and in our ongoing life journey we can transform these into opportunities for our own growth. To be able to take care of others we need to take care of ourselves: making space and time for whatever rejuvenates, accepting of life's challenges as opportunities, regular exercise, creative pursuits and time in Nature.

Jill, age 82.

I am my father's daughter
And do you know what that means?
He was filled with kindness
And fulfilling others dreams
I take his name now and always
Never will it change
It is the least I can do for the man
Who for his life I will rearrange
I will show gratitude and courage
For all that I have learnt
I will respect his wishes
Forever they can be taught
He saved so many people
With the love that he gave
I will attempt to emulate
The sacrifices he made
And until I become worthy
Of the name that I was born to
I will strive to be a better person
Today always and for you
I am my father's daughter
And do you know what that means?
He was filled with love
And fulfilling all of our dreams

For my father Mick Cox

Kellie M Cox

Be loyal to your friends (and football club).

Riley

Cats, yoga and boys who don't go to church.

As I too approach a milestone birthday, I've been setting new goals and generally taking stock. I've had a big change up over the past few years and now think the only good reason to look back is to see how far we've come. So, looking back now, I see the influence of the people, places, events, and even habits on my life. My husband, my son, family, and friends. A daily practice that keeps my feet on the ground and somehow my head in the clouds at the same time. Going vego a few years ago. The beach. Travel. What makes us who we are? Are we simply the sum total of our experiences?

Our parents are usually our first and greatest influence. My mum taught me a lot about what it means to be a mum; to love unconditionally, to teach discipline, to work hard to provide for a family. In my family home, there was always a bed for anyone who needed a place to crash and a meal for anyone who dropped in. We didn't have much in the way of material things, but mum was very good at making sure everyone had enough. She was fair. She taught me the importance of humility and keeping a sense of humour. Dad taught me intangible things like the importance of a good work ethic, of reading, of education.

When I became a parent, I called on much of what they taught, but as I approach the second half of my life, life's second act, what I like to think of as 'the juicy part,' I see how very different my life is from theirs. My parents weren't necessarily wrong, and they had only my best interests at heart, but we had some differences of opinion. They had plans for me, dreams, and expectations, and I let them down in almost every way.

These differences have had long ranging impacts on my life and can be boiled down to just three things; Cats, Yoga, and boys who don't go to church.

Firstly, there's cats. What is it about the fuzzy, little guys that makes us loathe them or love them utterly? Like most kids, I was an animal lover. I spent my first 5 years on a small farm, and we had everything from chickens and budgies to a small herd of Brahman cattle. We had a dog that was half dingo who would make her way to the local abattoir and steal a steer's head, dragging it back and clearing the six-foot chain wire fence and gnaw on it for days. We had cats, too. One deranged cat would hide under Mum and Dad's bed and swipe at our ankles as we ran down the hallway. Dad said it went mad from licking at the creosote on the stumps under the house.

Over the years many strays found their way to our door, but they never seemed to stay around for long. Dad wasn't a cat person. It took me until my mid 30s to understand the reason we could never keep a cat was that dad would move them on. The dislike of cats became a family trope, a story we all told ourselves about ourselves.

When my first husband was killed in a car accident, a friend bought me a kitten. It was an odd thing to do by today's standards. To be honest, I think it was an odd thing to do back then, too. I only found out years later about the kitten. She kept him. My mother told her it was a bad idea because we had never really had much luck with cats and losing the kitten, as I apparently, inevitably would, would just cause me more pain.

I don't know, it's a sliding doors moment, I suppose. Who knows what might have been if I'd really discovered how much I love cats in my early 20s? My cats, Ginger and George, and their predecessor, Bailey, are so precious to me. I grew up with dogs, I love dogs, but cats just get me somehow. I became vegetarian in an instant after losing Bailey. I asked myself, 'how can I mourn the death of one animal and go on contributing to the death of countless others?' Cats changed my life.

Speaking of life-changing, that brings me to yoga. I remember being so sublimely happy after my very first yoga class at university in 1990. Never a sporty person, I felt I had finally found *my* physical activity. Some stretching, balancing, and bending, followed by a nice lie down? What's not to love? I went home on a total high and wanted to share my experience with Mum because she had always suffered with physical and nerve pain and some anxiety issues. I thought she could benefit from yoga too. Mum, however, did not think yoga was a healthy thing to do. She was angry at me. Although I was 19, she made me promise I wouldn't return to the class. She didn't explain why, and I didn't ask.

I also didn't obey.

As I said, these were different times, I couldn't Google 'why is Yoga bad,' (Try it, it's a hoot.) After doing a bit of digging, I realise now Mum was convinced I would be brainwashed into a cult. After many years of yoga, my life is Exhibit A of the absolute opposite. If I do say so myself, yoga has given me strength of body and mind, emotional intelligence, and a calmness friends often comment on. Mum was right in a way; I am a different person because of yoga.

So, mum and dad were dead wrong about cats and yoga, but had I discovered goats and hiking, my life would be, could be, equally wonderful. If my sliding door moment had been fostering a rescue goat and discovering a hiking group, then I would be just as happy. But those boys who don't go to church are definitely a gift from some god or goddess somewhere.

Guilt, I've found, is the major export of the church. As a young teenager, I was legitimately terrified for a good few weeks that I would be 'chosen' by God for a virgin birth. It was only when I asked mum about it, through tears, and she laughed and laughed, that I relaxed on the subject. A lot of adopted kids feel they are 'here' for a reason and I was dead scared that reason was to give birth to a returning Christ. Anyone who knows me well will find that riotously funny. For years I was worried that my health problems were a punishment for going out with the wrong boy. I'd had a few admirers at church and did eventually go on a date with one of them. He drove a nice car and had a good job. He came from a good family. But let me just say, Mum simply didn't realise that most teenage boys have one thing on their minds and church it ain't.

So, in 1997 I married a man who has rarely set foot inside a church, not even for our wedding, and I've never regretted it. He's kind, generous and funny. Life is wonderful. My cats, my yoga, my boys who don't go to church (including my son) fill my days with laughter and joy. Imagine if I'd been the good girl who did everything the "right" way instead of my own way. I took my own path full of fluffy kitties, yoga retreats, and Sunday sleep ins and, to paraphrase the famous poem, that has made all the difference.

Christine Betts, Writer, age 50. @writerpainter

GOING WITHIN, LEARNING THE LESSONS AS LIFE THROWS THEM AT YOU

Everything happens for a reason. Well, that is one thought anyway. It is one that I do believe, and I have touched on some reasons for this in early chapters. I am a big believer in resilience and the growth mindset. I also know looking back after fifty years of doing a lot of things the hard way, that life will throw you the lessons that you need to learn. You might not always know the reason at the time, and they might feel impossible to get through and some will be.

Some situations and life lessons will rip your heart from your body. They will shake your every resolve. They will require every ounce of strength to get through. But you will, until the day when you no longer can.

No one promised us an easy life. Think back and reflect for a second, did anyone, every say to you… "Here is the next so many years of life as you know it, and it's going to be a breeze, cruise through, see you are the other end."

I think a more fitting description would be, "Here is your life, I am not going to tell you how long it is or who you are going to be journeying it with, but I can tell you, it will be a rollercoaster, some days you will be on top of the world and other days you will have fallen so far, you can't even see the top anymore. But when the ride is over, it's over, and you won't when that is happening either. So enjoy!"

Maybe the way we achieve such a feat as to last that rollercoaster ride is that we are not all in the same carriage at the same time. Maybe, when I am at the heading up to the peak of the summit, the sun shining on my face, the wind blowing, the view from the height absolutely breathtaking. Is it possible, that in that moment, I look down and see you plunging towards the ground, the terror of your face telling the story of immense fear of the unknown; your knuckles clenching the rail for some sense of safety, terrified beyond belief of the next pass the carriage is about to take.

Is it possible that in that moment, I look down and yell back to you, "It gets better, just hang in there!" And is it possible when the roles are reversed that you yell down to me, "Just keep moving, you will get through it!" Is it possible that is how we get through this roller coaster? We are all not in the depths of terror and despair at the same time. Nor are we all at the height of immense success and good fortune at the same time. At any time, we are at the lowest low, or the greatest high or anywhere in between. That on any given day, we are each in a different carriage, joined by different friends and family and propelled along at what feels like the speed of light toward the inevitable end of the ride.

Sometimes, someone slips out of the carriage, never to return. Sometimes, the carriages stop for just a second for a new life to join in the ride. Sometimes people move between carriages, they might stay with you for a short time or all of the ride. But one thing remains the same, the ride has dizzying heights and terrifying depths and once onboard it doesn't go backwards, only forwards at a speed that cannot be controlled.

Now I wish someone had explained life to me in these terms when I was younger. If I had this analogy of life and what it would look like, I wouldn't have spent the time I did looking backwards, worrying about what I did wrong. That part of the track is far behind me and I am never to return to it, to do it over again. I wouldn't fear the great descent that gathers speed making me feel as if I am about to get smashed on the hard ground, because after the fall, there is a slowing down, a levelling out before the next great high. If I had thought of this analogy earlier, I would have kept my focus more on the great heights I was to enjoy, waiting for the moment that carriage slipped into the sunshine, and allow myself to take in every aspect of the view from the amazing peak of the rollercoaster.

I am happy at least to realise this at fifty. Wow, maybe I am wiser with age! I plan to live to one hundred, that's the goal anyway, so I am according to my grand plan, only half-way through the rollercoaster ride of life. How about if I promise you this...that when I am heading skywards, I will look down and check on you, if you promise to do the same for me. I will yell down, "You will get through this!' and you yell back the same for me. Does that sound like a promise we can make?

I recently had a bit of sadness in my life, and I recall saying to a close friend, "I just have to stay with it. I just have to move through it, it feels like I am dragging my butt through quicksand and failing miserably, but I just have to keep moving one step at a time. There is no way out but through it."

This reminds me of something another close friend often says and wanted to share but couldn't as they weren't her own words. But her reminder goes something along the lines of swishy swashy, just move through the long grass. When I was having my sad time, I actually thought of these words. I am guessing at that point when my carriage was plummeting and I couldn't see the sunshine, my friend must have been above me yelling out, "Swishy swashy! Swishy swashy!"

My advice for life in this chapter is in two parts. One I have touched on earlier but is worth a reminder. The first is that life will be shite at times. Yes, she will kick you so hard in the stomach, you won't even be able to catch your breath, you will be alone in that moment and feel a dizzying pain in your head and a sickness to your stomach. But it won't last and then she will pick up you again, brush you off and take you on the most magical of adventures. Wow, I just realised, why people say, Life is a Bitch. She really is, isn't she!

The second part of my advice…is that true resilience is not just about standing back up after that kick in the stomach. It is about standing up, taking a deep breath and learning next time to move the other way before she kicks out again. It is about, finding the lesson in the tough stuff. It is about becoming a better, stronger, smarter you through what you have overcome. And it is in the great words of my mentor, finding the serendipity in life. Finding the good in the bad. The fortune in the most unfortunate of situations and remember to always be looking skywards for the sunshine.

I hope you enjoy the written pieces from my friends. The first piece is one I haven't yet worked out. My friend, Mark shared this analogy with me one day and I have been trying to understand it ever since. Even now, ten years or so later. One day I will get it. Until then, I hope you all enjoy!

Kellie M Cox

There's A Hole In Your Bucket
A Trilogy

Part 1:
When there is a hole in your bucket, you can choose to keep filling it up with water. The outcome will be yours to own.

Part 2:
The more holes in your bucket the easier the water will run out. You can keep doing the same thing to keep the water level up…if you choose…focusing on all of the emptiness as a whole can lead the bucket to being hollow and in that state it will remain.

Part 3:
You can focus on and fix one hole at a time and even slowly close the holes when you can, the outcome will be yours to own, and in that state it will remain.

Mark Simmons, Psychologist.

My Most Important Life Lesson I Learned From My Dog Olive

So, I liked to take my dog Olive for walks by the Brisbane River where she could run off leash. The problem was, if I let her run more than about 10 metres away from me without calling her back, she would bugger off and I wouldn't know where she was. It was like there was this line and once she crossed it, I would have absolutely no control over her. I could call and call and even though I knew she could hear me, she wouldn't come.

I realised one day that my Mind was like that too!

Something would happen and my mind would start making up stories about what was going to happen next - my kid was late home, and I would end up planning a funeral; my boss looked at me sideways and I would be thinking I was going to get the sack; my mum didn't answer her phone, she must have died in her sleep etc, etc.

Sometimes the stories were good, sometimes bad, sometimes they were like a disaster movie but all they were, were stories, they weren't real. The problem was my emotions didn't understand that they were just stories, and I would feel all the emotions I would feel if they had been real, so my internal life was a giant roller coaster - it was exhausting!

I decided to treat my mind like I treated Olive and each time it started to run away with a story I would call it back, so it never could get too far, and I wouldn't lose control.

It took me quite a number of years of practice to keep my mind walking quietly beside me, or when it started to run off with a story to be able to easily call it back.

Boy was it worth the effort! No more roller coaster, my days are lived in the present, dealing with what is in front of me, not some imagined reality. Very occasionally my mind will make up some story and I notice it quickly and usually find it amusing but the stories don't rule my life anymore.

Olive is dead now, she lived to the ripe old age of 14 but I'm forever grateful to her for the lesson that completely changed my life for the better.

Deb, age 70.

Don't waste time and energy thinking the grass is greener on the other side.

It took me a long time to learn the lesson that the grass is not always greener on the other side and the impact on my life has been dramatic. Did you ever wonder if the grass is greener on the other side? If so, then perhaps it is time to stop wasting thoughts and energies on this. There will always be pros and cons of everything no matter what you do or where you go.

When I lived near a capital city in a cooler climate, my parents took us interstate to a warmer regional town for holidays. I loved walking along the beach through sea-spray filled skies just as the sun was going down with my toes melting into the velvet sand. I told my parents I wanted to move to this area. Years later, my parents moved the family there, just a few minutes away from a beautiful surf beach. It was an exciting and wonderful time. I even got myself a surfboard.

A few years after the move though, I began missing the cooler weather, old buildings, character and culture that the big city offered. I made the interstate move back there on my own and slid into the bliss of late-night lattes down quaint secret alleyways, walking down pathways strewn with autumn leaves set in beautiful wide city streets heavily lined with maple and oak trees.

But my family were back in the seaside town, and I missed its warm welcoming waters, and hiking through the nearby beautiful pristine subtropical rainforest.

I ended up doing the move back and forth between the big vibrant city and the regional town multiple times. Why? Because although it appeared the grass was greener on the other side, it never was. Both places offered completely different experiences and both places had pros and cons that were significant. It took me a very long time of living with *the grass is greener* syndrome to come to terms with certain facts. That is, that I could be equally happy in either place if I just put my time and energy into focusing on all the great things the location that I actually lived in had to offer.

I no longer think of what I am missing from not living in a diverse capital city, I just focus on the wonderful pros of living in a warm regional area.

It has been the same with being single versus being married or working from the office versus working from home. Time and energy spent thinking the *grass is greener on the other side* is wasted and pointless. Adapt to your situation, focus on the pros, and use your time and energy for something more constructive and pleasurable rather than ever imagining you are missing out on something better. The grass isn't greener, it's just a different type.

Tracey Winning

My Story begins in 1980, when I was hit by a car in East Devonport Tasmania while waiting on the side of the road with my Mother. After fighting for my life in hospital for a period which spanned several months, I pulled through to be here today. However, my fight for life had only just began with Hemiplegia/Cerebral Palsy and an acquired brain injury. My Mother consistently annoyed me with rehabilitation programs which has enabled me to fulfill my dreams and goals in life today. However, when she passed away beside me in another car tragedy, I was left to my own devices to find my own way in the world and had to rely on the support of my other family members. Therefore, creating a close relationship with them took time.

My friends saw me struggle through High School and onto years 11 & 12, however I was awarded an award at the end of year 12 for my achievements. This enabled me to study hospitality at a College in Launceston Tasmania and received the young citizen of the year award for Devonport in the year 2000 for my achievements with Swimmers with a Disability. Each month I would represent Tasmania in disability swimming events in NSW for a period of 10 years, winning the National Gold in 2000. In 2004, I joined the State Labor Party and in 2008 - 2013 I was an independent candidate at the local government elections for Devonport Tasmania as I wanted to feel I had a purpose in local society. As one of my goals and dreams was to move to Queensland I was secretly applying for rental properties (without the knowledge of my family) in Brisbane where I had helpful supportive friends.

After receiving news that I had secured a rental property in Brisbane in November 2017, I told my family who were shocked. After two years in Brisbane, I then fulfilled my dream of moving to the Gold Coast to continue completing my list of Dreams and Goals and in 2019 I was awarded the Syd Phillips Memorial Trophy for winning a Toastmasters Poetry competition and in 2020 I also was the runner up for reciting my own self written poetry. Another one of my goals and dreams was to become an Actor, so in 2019 I also applied to study acting for film at the Gold Coast Film Academy and was accepted. This was a goal and dream I had for 22 years which I listed on my vision board 22 years ago. I'm so grateful to be trained in Creative Studies, Voice and Speech, Technique and Scene Study Analysis. Recently I performed a 5-week stage production of Bye Bye Birdie at the Gold Coast Little Theatre and was in a film as a bullied man in a movie called The Lost One and also filming a documentary about my Journey in Queensland.

My life's journey has taught me that everything happens for a reason. I need to live in the moment so that I can reach my goals and dreams in life. Together with trusting in the moment cause all of us are exactly where we need to be.

As Helen Keller said..."It has been said that life has treated me harshly and sometimes I have complained in my heart because many pleasures of human experience have been with-held from me. If much has been denied from me, much, very much, has been given to me."

Damian McCoy, Actor, Model, Speaker.

My Advice to My Younger Self - Always Follow Your Intuition and Premonition!

I remember my 50th birthday like yesterday. My soulmate of twenty years at that time, had asked me to wear my finest clothes for that evening. He was taking me out to dinner in the swishiest restaurant in town, to celebrate both my birthday and our twenty-year marriage.

I did just that, I wore the latest fashion night blue taffeta cocktail dress with a wide decollate that accentuated my neckline; it had short puffy sleeves and a wide belt for my small waist; I complimented my beautiful dress with a matching blue purse with silver chain that I latched on to my wrist. I wore open high heel silver sandals. The exquisite silver diamonds and sapphire necklace with matching clip-on earrings I wore, I had inherited from my grandmother. With perfectly applied make-up, manicured nails and professional coiffured hair in the style of the seventies, the years of the big hair, I felt like a Princess, sort of wearing a tiara.

I was excited at the prospect of a night out with my soulmate, but my intuition and premonitions told me to be on my guard.

It had been raining heavily that afternoon, and on arriving at our destination my soulmate parked the car under the protective canopy above the restaurant's entrance. The doorman rushed to open the driver's side door first; he then came around to my side, and with a respectful bow, he opened the car door for me. In doing that he accidently bumped the car door on the pole holding up the canopy, allowing the rain water to cascade and drench the one person standing right below it, me! I felt the cool of the water travel from the top of my head down my back under my dress all the way down my legs and on to my fee. The doorman stood stone-faced waiting for my reaction; my instinct told me to ignore it, a Lady does not make a scene for a little bit of water, and proudly holding on to my soulmate's arm we walked into the restaurant with my feet making a squishing sound.

There was a sense of quiet mystique; you could almost hear a pin drop, as we entered the softly dimmed restaurant. The maître d with a pure while linen napkin over his left arm and the right arm elegantly bent behind his body, was making small talk of welcome while escorting us to our table. With the expertise of a man who has done that numerous times, the maître d pulled the chair out for me to sit down. On the centre of the table covered by a pure white tablecloth there was a garland of red rosebuds holding up an emerald green coloured candle.

The maître d lit the candle and asked if it was a special night for us; and could he suggest something special, the most expensive important bottle of wine on the list. My soulmate agreed to the recommendation and the maître d called over one of the waiters to attend to our service. All of this being said with subdued whispers that gently echoed in the empty restaurant. I looked around; it was set with approximately ten round tables. Each table was set with the finest china and decorated with garlands of red rosebuds and emerald candles; I noticed that the crystal flutes were also of green colour, everything was matching our table. Half dozen waiters were discreetly lined up at the ready, but they had no one to serve. The water tank with live lobsters looked very impressive and in a secluded corner a solo violinist in dinner suit commenced to play our favourite song. I commented to my soulmate how romantic he was, even after twenty years, to have the restaurant all to ourselves, just like on our very first dinner date. He lovingly held my hand and told me he remembered that my second favourite colour is green and that is the colour that represents twenty years wedding anniversary, and it was our blessed anniversary.

My heart was filled with love, but I was feeling a little uncomfortable from the drenching I had received, and while we waited for our drinks, I excused myself and made my way to the Ladies room. On entering into the bright light of the elegant restroom the mirror revealed the extent of my predicament!

The back of my beautiful night blue taffeta gown was made to look much darker than the front, almost black by the water. The puffed sleeves were deflated, and my perfectly professionally big, coiffured hair was now looking like a pancake sitting on top of my head. I tried my very best to revive my puffy sleeves and hairdo, to make it sit up again, but the water had its most tragic effect. I had no choice; I accepted my fate; I fooled myself with thinking that my soulmate would not have noticed it because he loved me no matter how I looked.

Putting on a bright smile I almost waltzed to our table relieved to see how subdue the light was, the waiters had not noticed my disheveled appearance. Again, the maître d who had been standing at a safe distance came over to hold my chair. The moment I sat down the double doors of the restaurant opened up and a crowd of fifty people I recognised as our friends came in shouting "Surprise, surprise" and singing Happy Birthday for me!

Suddenly, I wanted to disappear from everyone's view! Having to explain to each of my girlfriends what had happened, was a task I was not looking forward to, when once again the intuition and premonition that has guided me all my life took over.

Among the cheers and hand claps I stood up and they all went quiet, waiting for a speech from me. I casually opened my elegant handbag, pulled out my tiara and placed it on top of my pancake. In silence, every man bowed, and every lady curtsied, followed by a long roaring laughter while listening to my soulmate tell what happened, in such a way that made the event sound like a love letter from him to me. Everyone enjoyed the night, most of all, me.

The moral of the story is; no matter how careful you are on your life's travels, something is bound to go wrong. Always be prepared, follow your intuition and premonition, you never know when you may need to wear your tiara.

**Livia York, The Poetic Phoenix, Published
Author/Poetess/Public Speaker/Singer Entertainer.**

JUST DO YOU!

Just do you. One of my favourite quotes I like to post is "Other people's opinion of you, is none of your concern." I am well aware that this notion is much easier to say than to do. I think I wrote this, after one day being in the kitchen with my adult son, who didn't like something I was saying and replied with, "You are entitled to your opinion, but I just don't need to hear it." It might sound harsh but bear with me here. I raised my kids to think independently, and I am so incredibly happy that they are the adults they are today.

Even the most innocent of meals around our table can be a start of another great debate. If there is a candle in middle of the table, one person will say it is blue, one person will say it is red and one will argue that the candle only actually exists in our imagination. I kid you not. One person, who joined us for a family lunch around the pool, got up sighing to himself while he said, "you people are exhausting!"

In fact, not too long ago, we adopted a healthy behaviour strategy that we call the Blair effect. The technique is to simply… JUST WALK AWAY. My son, when he has had enough of a conversation that is irritating him, or more often than not boring him, or a person that is irritating (or more likely boring) him, will simply get up and leave the room. He doesn't storm out, he doesn't ask permission, he just stands up and unforgivingly walks away. He returns when he hears something of interest, or the conversation has moved on. The girls in the family have loved this technique and some have even tried it out for themselves. When you don't want to be somewhere, just walk away. How liberating would that be. Why don't we do that more?

Why do we get so caught up in what is expected of us or other people's opinions that we leave ourselves in situations that don't serve us or around people that are simply not good for us at that point in time? A wise friend once asked me, "if you don't respect a person, why would you respect their opinion?" I initially reacted with the growth mindset mentality of the learnings that come from people who are different to us. But my friend corrected me and said, "It isn't about people who are different, it is about people who you hold no regards or respect for."

This ideal does not speak to hurting another or disrespecting another but simply about respecting yourself more than others. It is about staying true to who you are. I recently had to grade a student with a not yet competent after a practical assessment and her immediate response was, "I respectfully disagree." I tried not to smile, because I had never heard a student say that before. I replied with, "You can disagree, but I still can't grant you a competent and here is why." I went on to explain and hope that some of what I shared was helpful for future assessments.

We have touched on what it means to find beauty, live with passion, demonstrate great courage, learn from life, challenge ourselves and create family. At the end of all of that we explore the concept of just being you. Being the uniquely capable, beautiful, brilliant you that only you can be.

I worked as a counsellor in a creative college working with students studying film, acting and screenwriting. As part of the induction process, I was to introduce myself and share what supports I could offer as they embark on their studies. It was difficult not to also offer some advice. One saddening thing I would see with each new group was that as the group dynamics started to form, the students began to label themselves and assign themselves grades. This was never something done by the lecturers but by the students themselves. "I am only ever going to be the funny fat girl," is what one student told me. Another reported that their classmates assigned them to the role of good-looking action hero and nothing more. They had pigeonholed themselves into an assigned role that their society - their class had created for them. Never did I hear a student talk to me about wanting to be typecast but instead wanting to learn and challenge themselves and play roles outside of their comfort zone. But within the short few weeks of what many envisage to be a lifelong career, they had begun to own their assigned societal labels.

Many students coming straight out of secondary education spoke of their position in the grading of the class and to understand why this wasn't even possible, was that assessments were graded. The marking was being done purely from the audience of student learners who needed the comfort of finding out if they were top of the class, middle or bottom. Is there a sense of security knowing our place in our surroundings? Does it give comfort that once assigned, you are no longer having to work towards the achievement of greatness? At the end of the day, I put it down to our education system and the ranking that is required to award tertiary placements. But what if you are a student always told you are a C grade student. Where is the motivation or even, the thought that you could strive for more, if indeed you wished for that.

So, my advice to new students as I spoke to them at their induction was simply, "Just be you! You have gained a place in this learning institution based on how you uniquely are. You will write a script, direct a movie or play a character as only you can. Just trust that unique quality of you and let that creativity drive you to do the best you can."

As a part of this project, Advice For Life, I asked the contributors if they wanted to share their occupation or age or anything that is relevant to their written piece and gives some context to where their advice for life comes from. Some of my favourite labels were - healer, working mother of two and trailblazer and entrepreneur. As adults we tend to meet each other and ask, "What do you do?" It might sound a little quirky, but what if we asked, "Who are you?" I wonder what different responses we would get.

As a creative coach, I hear a lot of the imposter syndrome. Whether it is from writers, actors, filmmakers, it is always the same. I recently even heard it within a group of newly graduated counsellors. My response to that is, you are simply you. You will write words that people will want to hear. Not everyone, but the readers who find your work, will love it and remain loyal to your publications. The clients who mesh and build rapport with you as a counsellor, will be your clients. If they don't, it is simply a matter of them finding the right clinical support for themselves. We need enough of every occupation out there so that when people are looking, they find the right person for them.

There were again, so many written pieces that fitted with this heading, but I couldn't put all of them into this one chapter. The friends who contributed to this book, truly do live by the motto, JUST DO YOU! Hope you enjoy their pieces.

Kellie M Cox

Advice for Life

In a nutshell, I don't have any, rather, you must live your own life.

Life will deliver a whole list of "ifs" and the choices or decisions we make can impact on our life within the blink of an eye, define us forever?

Throughout life's journey, we will face challenges and obstacles, take risks, make mistakes and hopefully learn from them, sometimes lose our way, seek and embrace happiness and enjoy special moments.

In saying that, when I think back to myself as a naïve 20-year-old, leaving home to get married and start a new life, to now at the age of 70, those 50 years (Kellie's age) have been a great journey and my personal growth immeasurable. I am certainly not the same person as I was back then, and very thankful with where I am, no regrets and would not do anything different to what I have done in the past.

Therefore, I can't give advice on what you should do, you have to do it yourself, but enjoy the ride!!

Sharon, age 70.

Young people shouldn't rush in to settle down, get married and have children too early these days. They should travel and do everything they want to do and then later on when they have done everything, then they are ready to settle down.

Margaret Cox, age 81.

"My dear, we are writers.
We must partake of whatever devilish desires our little hearts crave.
It is what allows our artistic juices to flow."

Kellie M Cox
A line from Daniel in the novel, **Murderous Intent**.

Poem For Kellie

Words leave
upon arriving,
another breath
and they're gone.
Carry a notebook.
Write everything down.

Let everyone
be the monarch
of their own
kingdom of feelings!

Ideas perfect
in the mind
break on being born.
The space between
you
and your ideal
is the shape
of your beauty.

Live your life
like a lighthouse:
stand tall,
shine,
be a light for lost travellers.

You are a spirit
made material -
do not believe the mirror.
You are elsewhere.

Do not fight the war
in every battle.
Do not trust
the council.

You cannot hear the wind.
But from the sound of the leaves
you hear the wind.

Work grinds
you a lens
through which
you see the world.

When you say
to your child
what was said
to you
time punctures
to a pinhole
through which you can
crawl
and parent yourself.
When you return
to this time
give what you found
to your child.

Wayne Hasselman

Anything you're putting off is not going to get better with time.
Choosing not to do something is still a choice.

Sarah

Excuse Me While I See Things Differently

I have a wallpaper on my phone as a daily reminder. It reads:
"I need to stop acting like I am afraid of my own power and start to move as my highest self, completely and unapologetically. "
I have spent several years teaching others how to do this and yet, I am the one who requires this advice the most.
For I was a child of conformity until I recently remembered that I am a 'volunteer', a Star-seed Earthling who has been forging a path, finding her voice, and observing the way the Universe and humans behave in mystically unreasonable ways.

We all want things to always work out for us – our way.
We scrutinise our decisions and our choices based on the opinions of others as if this were a chose your own adventure story.
WE NEED TO STOP PLAYING IN THE STORY LINES!
There is no easy way around this life you are here to live.
The only way is through it.
Balancing living fearlessly, holding the line, holding onto your free will and freedom.
Having courage to stand in the fire without the fear of it burning you.
When you are unconditionally Loving out loud
Loving your darkness and your light.
Learning that dark places are a space of amazing creations, not the monsters under the bed.
The darkness is the only place where you see the light in the form of deepest gratitude.
A realisation we are connected to everything.
The void is never empty but full of opportunity to celebrate all that you are, all that you
have and all that you are yet to become.
This is a strange question but ....
When did you last consider your connection to the paint on the walls of your home, the fibres of the carpet?
Could you count the amount of people who had a hand in the process of the making to the final application?

The stories they could tell you. These inanimate objects that would not be in existence and in your proximity without several human life stories touching it!

Going back to the origins of everything around you that you are familiar with every day, yet
strangers, and infinite web of strangers made this all possible for you. This is the deepest for of gratitude imaginable. Here lies the freedom and the joy you seek.
To know that without our connection to each other – nothing would exist.

Yet we insist on focusing on our differences.
From birth our humanness becomes measured and weighed and our milestones assessed
and compared to a bar set as "normal."
We are told that we are unique until it's not ok to celebrate your uniqueness.
We strive for equality, but we all want to be the loudest voice of our campaign.
Un willing to be uncomfortable with the truth that being equal creates a level playing field
and there can be NO minority and hierarchy?
Could we truly be existing in a world like this as we are now without our stories?
While we struggle to be heard we forget that the greatest law of attraction is friendship.
Observing our differences with curiosity, compassion, and kindness.
Daring to wear our own style, using our diversity to captivate and educate.
With tolerance and love – experiencing the sheer joy of our own existence being in this now
moment on this earth plane that we volunteered for whether we know this or not.
Recollections of sovereignty, self-esteem, self-worth, self-confidence, self-love as we remember our childhood innocence as we blow out each candle on our adulting anniversary wrestling with our selfish ego that this year will be different. It will be MY year. This will be the story that keeps repeating as we wait for this to be reasonable and perfect.

Our imagination fooled us into believing that we would be free once we had grown but we find ourselves trapped by our own expectation of reality, that nothing is perfect and perfect at the same time. You are playing your part without knowing the story line or the script.

Before your soul came into this human form you made several sacred contracts with others who hold the tools, the wisdom and the lessons in little backpack and you agreed to carry theirs. You know them as soon as you meet them again. There are no coincidental connections. There is no fate just divine, spiritual faith that this adventure will equip you with everything you need to complete your earth side purpose with these guides, soulmate, fellow star seeds and universal adventurers full of their human stories and wounds.

These tend to be the moments of our lives that bring great change, destruction, and upheaval as we prepare to give up who you think you are and the plot twist in the story line become apparent. You lose hope, gain weight, forget to love yourself and buy into the tabloid fake news about yourself that's stuck on repeat, nightly at 6 when you're home alone with your stuff and the bullshit feeling emotionless and numb knowing that we have been holding onto this like an old pillow because it's safer and comfortable here and my story has become my excuse not to be greater. Not to be powerful. That would make me responsible for every lie I tell myself that I am.

I want to share the way I have hacked I learned from my spiritual guides that have help me release these lies, negative thoughts, feelings, trauma and emotions that have been weighing me down in hope that it serves you a powerful visualisation to help you do the same.

I invite you to imagine a trauma, a negative feeling or experience you believe makes up a part of who you are a story that no longer serves you and imagine this in the shape of a ships anchor.

As soon as you feel these things, you make the choice to release as opposed to trying to figure it out or analyse it, attaching a judgement or story line to it. Instead of doing this you grab it and release it down into the earth as far as you can and when it is deeply anchored, cut the anchor chain free and

At the exact same moment, I want you to step into body with your breath in the now
moment as you embody the version of yourself without those attachments, releasing all the

old versions of you that have not been serving you for a long time.
Often when you feel these emotions and trauma patterns that have been with you and
following you for a long time, we have the knee jerk reaction to judge it and blame others.
Replacing this behaviour with a choice to be in your sovereign higherstate will help you
regain your personal power of choice.
This simple hack allows you to bring yourself back into the present moment and instantaneously release this pattern of thoughts and feelings if you believe and chose this to
work for you. It has allowed me greater understanding and compassion for those who test me and think
differently to the way I do making their judgements and thoughts about me less personal and more toward my truth. With practice I hope this allows you to do the same.

****

My contribution to this incredible collection of life advice celebrates stepping into my power
and moving as my highest self, completely and unapologetically leaving behind 50 years of feeling like I did not belong because I saw life differently. My intention for you Kellie and the future readers of this book is to recognise the light of one human who discovers their truth has been lighting that human existence for thousands of years. Such is the power of a human being who finally realises the truth of who they are.

Archetype Junkie, included): Personal Truth Inquirer, Emotional Baggage handler and Mystically Unreasonable Intuitive Therapist - 50.5 earth side, @archetype_junkie

My simple life reflections.
"Believe in you...and always find that glimmer of hope"
"Remember those low points when you survived...you did it then,
you will do it again"

"Never forget the joy of laughter...no matter what anyone thinks"

Svetlana Jankowiak

Totally Inhabit the Life We Have

We each have a unique experience of life. We can accept and embrace that life fully, or we can wish and hope it was different; and at times struggle against whatever is uncomfortable, difficult or even traumatic. Each of us have awareness of the many factors that lead us to the feelings, desires, reactions, avoidances, longings and sometimes addictions that we know are part of who we are.

However, to totally inhabit the life we are living right now, we must take responsibility for who we are and who we want to be.

In my understanding, we must totally accept everything about ourselves without any judgement. That doesn't mean staying the same. We choose what to continue, cease, change, or develop further. And at times we might want to make amends when our own behaviour harms ourselves or another.

Be grateful for who we are, who is in our lives, and all present circumstances. Welcome the difficult and painful stuff that you can't avoid, along with the successful and joyful experiences. Face it with self belief and courage; even if you have to 'Fake it till you make it' in some situations.

Hold onto a belief that every intention, goal, dream, and door that can open, can be reached from here. Choose what to persevere with and what to let go of.

I'd rather focus on what really works in a situation to the best of my ability, than on what is supposed to be right or wrong; I'd rather come to understand and live by my truth (acknowledging that it might change in a month or a year).

For me, it's a work in progress; and would not be possible without reflection, meditation and mindfulness. That might be deliberate practice, or just time in the garden or bush, or walking casually without any particular thought process. In fact, I value having regular time to be 'Out of my Mind'.

Although our own life here is unique, I don't believe we are at all separate. Recognise the connections; and know there is support, wisdom, and inspiration always available. We just need to be open to it.

Terry Pinney, retired, age 70.

DEATH... OR...WHATEVER WE BELIEVE HAPPENS

Death, or...as I like to suggest, whatever you believe happens, might actually happen.

Don't worry we won't end this book on a sad note with the topic of death, but it is inevitable. From the moment we are born we start dying and I've got a bit to do here yet, if I am planning on reaching the big 100!

I am halfway, so anything is possible. We end this journey of sharing of wisdom at the same place we began. It all comes back to love. For each time I see you, write you an email, send you a little heart at the end of a message that is me telling you, I love you and you are in my thoughts. That is me being present, of showing courage, of being kind and absolutely grateful of everyday we have here alive and well and being around people we care about.

As a new counsellor, I felt truly useless to my clients in the area of loss and grief, especially around bereavement. I have had to work hard over the years to develop a sense of practice that actually fulfils the client's needs. I am feeling much more confident now, and it only took me twenty years of practice to get there.

When a client talks to me about losing a loved one, I ask them one of two questions, "What did your loved one believe happens when they die?" or "What do you believe happens when you die?" The question I ask is dependent on the person and their situation. I have used this for many years now and I can tell you honestly, the response is always the same.

The client leans into me, they lower their voice to a whisper, and they share what they believe to be their wildest and hope-filled beliefs about life after death. They whisper, because up until now it has been their secret. The innermost thought that they dared not to share with the world. I am honoured to hear their answers. Some will speak of a life after death and being able to speak to their loved ones, often this occurs in dreams. Many responses relate to their loved ones sending them a sign - often it is in nature; an animal, a sunset, a rainbow, a butterfly. Many times, it can be through music; a song randomly played at just the time they needed to hear it. Although their behaviour is the same when they are sharing their secret, their beliefs about life and death are as varied and unique as they are.

I respond with this thought. "No one in the world has as far as we know it come back from the death and disproven what you have just suggested." This gives the client some evidence to support their heartfelt belief. I go on to suggest, "Maybe, whatever you believe happens for you or your loved ones, actually does happen. Maybe we get to choose and for each of us we choose something different. What if your mum got her wish and she would send you signs in the form of a butterfly; what if your father could speak to you in your dreams; what if your best friend does send you that song each time they see you need to hear it again?"

When you think about it, there is absolutely no way to disprove that any of this is possible. In the absence of a strong religious faith, people are sometimes left feeling as if they don't have an answer for life after death, but what if the outcome is whatever we want it to be?

My clients feel amazing comfort and confidence in the notion that their innermost beliefs may actually come true. Counselling is a safe and non-judgmental space where clients get to share these ideals with a professional. They share words they cannot say to even the closest of loved ones. To have their thought validated and supported is of immense encouragement.

We continue to session with, "What if we agree that this thing you believe happens, so you next see a butterfly, what are you going to say to your mother?" or "You know you can talk to your father in your dreams, what you do want to let him know?" I promise you this is the turning point in the session. Each client is able to share, what they want to say, how they are going to be prepared and even more aware of the signs and opportunities around them.

If their loved one is facing death, I might even ask the client what it would be like to share this conversation with their loved ones. Have they had this conversation before? Do you know what their loves ones are thinking about as they face the end? If the client is strong enough, I might even suggest they have this discussion with their loved one. Imagine, if you are alone in a hospital bed and knowing the end is near, what do you think you might be contemplating. I imagine a person might be wondering what happens when they die, if it will hurt, if they will even know when it happens.

What if a trusted loved one, in a quiet moment had the courage to give them the space to voice these beliefs and these fears. I cannot think of a more empowering and courageous act than to sit with a person in their final stretch of life and allow them to truly share their innermost thoughts they are sitting with every day.

A client returned for a second session after having this conversation about the death of his father. He shared with me, something that was truly inspiring. His teenage daughter had been missing her grandfather as well and he was able to start a conversation with her about what happens after death. He shared with me something amazing and something he thought to do entirely on his own. He told his teenage daughter that when he too passed, that she shouldn't feel any fear or sadness for him and that when she wanted to talk to him, she should just do exactly that. She should look skywards and say everything she wanted her father to know and that he would be listening. My client shared with me his belief, that he had just had the single most important conversation with his daughter that he would ever have in his life.

My practice development around bereavement came about in looking for diverse strategies to share with my clients. Much of the initial thought to do this came about after my chosen sisters and I all shared losses one after the after. Something good can come out of something bad and my friends and I all had funerals to attend for each other but also conversations of support, care and love. One wise friend who didn't have a religious or cultural context to death and grieving started researching ideas for each of us. For me she shared the Buddhist prayer of thanking a loved one for being in your life and wishing them well. This is done as soon as you hear of their passing.

It is so your loved one can feel free to say goodbye, the words they hear from you are around gratitude and love and hope.

For herself, this wise friend liked the idea of covering mirrors for a period after the death. Other strategies include planting a tree, writing a letter, lighting a candle (which we do together when we come across a beautiful old church.)

As I mentioned in the earlier chapter about love in all its forms, my father and I were extremely close. I spent much of my childhood following him around to his various jobs. I insisted every Sunday to visit Channel Seven studios at Mount Cootha where he was a television presenter. I would watch from behind the cameras at the hijinks happening on set. I would be in the race caller box while he was calling the races, even once tripped over the microphone cord mid race which stopped all calling until my dad could plug it back in again. I would play in the printing presses at The Courier Mail where he was the Advertising Manager and I would wake up in the dark of morning; my mother having laid out warm clothes for me at the end of my bed the night before to go to the racetrack with my father and our apprentice jockey to run track work with the thoroughbreds.

As an adult, I even worked for my father and when I become a mother myself, I would receive a call from him every Wednesday morning, when my mother went to the hairdressers. The call was an hour list of instructions and reminding me to mow the lawn and asking what the chlorine levels were in the pool and did I need him to come over and trim that frangipani tree at the front of the house. As a single parent, I used to have to take road trips for work but would insist on taking my two young boys. I remember I had to ring Dad to tell him when I was leaving, then ring when I reached my destination and then ring again the next day when I was leaving again and one final time when we all returned home safely. I used to think it was a little bit of overkill but I can tell you now that he is gone, I would give anything for an hour-long phone call with a list of instructions on the running of my house. I would even likely purposefully drag it to two hours.

It was through this closeness, that I had the courage one night when I had snuck in after hours to chat with Dad in the hospital, to ask him what he thought happened when he died. Dad was a catholic and believed that when he died, there was nothing but blackness. Your body was placed in the ground and nothing else happened after that. I couldn't believe this to be true. My father had such an energy, such a spirit for life and for people that I couldn't just believe that a spirit and energy so strong could be distinguished like that.

Dad must have seen my face and he asked me the same question. I had my answer. I knew what I wanted to happen when my much-loved father passed. I told him that an energy so strong doesn't just disappear, that it changes somehow. The energy of a soul lives on after the body has given up. I wasn't entirely sure what that looked like, but I was sure that I would still have the energy and love of my father in my life after he passed. He was too strong a human being for it to be any other way.

Dad was quick to respond. "You know what Kel? I will strive for that and if I can do it, I will send you a message. How about that?"

Well, you can probably already guess what happened next. It was months later, and I was at my wedding reception. My father had told my then boyfriend on his death bed, "You better be serious and marry her and not mess her around." So, in staying true to his promise, to my father, my partner did just that.

I was in the ladies' bathroom alone at the beginning of the small reception in Port Douglas. A few family and friends had joined us for the wedding in the small glass chapel on the beach. I was looking in the mirror adjusting my makeup, when my father's voice spoke to me loudly and clearly, "That was a beautiful ceremony Kel."

"Thanks Dad," I replied. "I am glad you were there."

I didn't mention a word of this to anyone, nor had I ever spoken to my family about the promise my father made to me that night in the hospital. It was less than fifteen minutes later, when my mother came up to me, a surprised look on her face. "Kel, you will never guess what happened in the ladies' bathroom." I smiled for I figured I already knew.

My mother went on to tell me that she had taken her very young grandson, my nephew to the bathroom only a short time earlier. She said that while in the bathroom he started talking to someone who wasn't there. When they exited the bathroom, he said "Goodbye Mickey." Now, my father's name was Mick, Michael or friends called him Mickey Cox. His grandson would have been too young to even know him as anything other than Grandad.

My mother was perplexed, and she asked her grandson who he was talking to and he replied "Grandad Mickey."

I got to share with my mother that I had spoken to Dad only a few minutes earlier. When I returned later in the day, he wasn't there. I imagine knowing him, he had many more people to watch over besides just me.

As the second last chapter of our little book, I needed to make mention of one of the toughest moments in life we will even face. I hope you have enjoyed my personal story and the words of wisdom to follow.

Kellie M Cox

how is this sadness
so real it penetrates
the soul
when the longing
refuses to cease
that it grips
at my heart
the loss of you
unimaginable in my
mind
yet the wise consciousness
knows more
for it sees that
although not seen
you are never
far from reach
always in my
mind, my heart
and my soul
until I see
you again
my only
you

Kellie M Cox

Fear of death

Only a couple of years ago this was my biggest terror. I would wake up in the still wee hours of the night in a fearful panic, lying in my bed staring out at the blackness. It was these moments when I felt the most insecure, the uncertainty of who I was beyond my body all-consuming my awareness. I was mostly convinced I would be annihilated upon taking my final breath. This largely stemmed from my religious upbringing, a deeply effective indoctrination that had once convinced me that I was a sinner destined to eternal damnation. This never made sense to my logical mind, nor aligned with the deep enquiry, research and investigation into religion and history that I later poured myself over. My solution; to abandon this for the other extreme – the belief in complete and utter annihilation.

In my early thirties my courageous baby brother was diagnosed with stage 4 melanoma cancer. I watched as his vitality slowly drained from his body, but never his lust for life. He had always been the family clown and practical joker and these qualities were only enhanced. It was six years and hundreds of hours of tears behind me when he finally left this world at the tender age of 33 years old. This journey became my biggest lesson. During his last years I began to open up the conversation to the taboo subject of death. I looked behind the veil of polite western suppressive culture and saw that others were talking about death too. I made it a mission to bring it out into my conscious awareness on a daily basis. I even downloaded a smart phone app that would send me five inspirational quotes about death each day. By then I had grown immensely in my emotional resilience, making it a priority to master my mind and face my fears. Whilst processing my grief I asked for help from a wonderful coach and counsellor who showed me that I might like to look at celebrating instead of mourning my brother's journey to the other side. I wasn't so sure still about the soul living on but I did take her comments on board and began to feel comforted. Only a week before he passed, I asked him very specifically if he would give me a sign when he was safe on the other side. I figured I had nothing to lose in this simple request and was relieved when he responded in the affirmative with enthusiasm. I recall thinking that his assuredness made me question if he knew something I didn't.

I received a call from my mum the morning of his death. It had been only ten minutes since he had taken his last breath. Stunned, I felt unusually still and peaceful as I allowed the news to sink in. This was the scary moment I had waited for, for six long years. I was distinctly aware that it wasn't the stab in my heart I had expected. Surprising, even to myself, I got in my car and decided to drive to work, a good hour's drive. I remember feeling a numbed kind of relief knowing he was out of his ailing body and finally free of his suffering. I turned on my favourite podcast series by Hay House and began the usual road trip to the next city where I was teaching a class of jobseekers emotional life skills. I turned up the volume and found a song was about to begin, a melodic and joyful guitar piece whistled through the speakers. Then two beautiful voices started singing just one word over and over again – "Celebration". Goosebumps shot up and down my arms and legs as I allowed the words to sink in. I recalled the conversation with my coach and counsellor and felt compelled to take in the message of celebration of a life lived so beautifully. I breathed into the words and felt deep joy, gratitude and appreciation for having known him and loved him.

When the song ended a woman's voice began to speak. She was the next inspirational speaker at a pre-recorded live event, and she was about to share her miraculous life-altering story with the audience. I listened as she first began describing being on death's bed in a hospital. As she spoke, she described in great detail all of the elements of her physical suffering. It struck me that every single deathly affliction she was depicting was the exact same symptoms my dear brother had faced in his last hours of life, in real time, only moments before. From the multiple tumours choking her organs to the edema that swelled up her body's tissues, all the while feeling the agony of intense insufferable pain. She then described leaving her body, moving up and becoming aware of her new form – that of the essence of pure unconditional love. There was no fear where she was, no terror and no grief. Once again, goosebumps entirely covered my skin as I suddenly realised that Mikey was talking to me. She was able to recall seeing her whole family making their way to the hospital to say goodbye to her. She could see her brother was not going to make it in time as he boarded an aeroplane. And then she was shown that she had an option this time, that it didn't have to be her time to go, that she could return and be healed and change millions of lives in the process. I sat back in my chair in the bumper-to-bumper traffic of the busy highway in awe. I felt the presence of my brother with me in the car, smiling at me. I smiled back. I knew he'd just given me the sign I'd asked for. He was safe on the other side. Fear of death is not a thing in my life anymore. Without that fear I live more fully, more joyfully and more peacefully. Accept death, love it and never deny it. Celebrate your life instead of fearing an end, for I believe, the end as we think we know it, never comes.

Malise Banks, Speaker, Coach & Counsellor, Trainer.

I've pondered for some time about the fundamental virtues which guide my life. Here is what I know to be true from my 56 years:

- Life is fleeting: embrace life, time is precious
- All things will pass: be it what you want to hold onto or let go
- Memento mori: remember, every day, that you will die
- Flow like water and bend like the wind: it's the Way
- Nature is beautiful: feel it, see it, touch it, hear it, taste it – be immersed
- Love, love, love: the Greek word agape encapsulates love for family, friends, communities in your sphere and beyond. Cultivate it, share it and value it.

Sunita

Suddenly, I died tonight
With a horrible thought
I've not done enough to make it right.

Our mother earth, her other souls
Then I remember our legacies
Beautiful children, lives not yet told.

And do you know why I am so sure?
It's because they are our hope
Our future...our only cure.

Kellie M Cox

Regret

Spend time with your loved ones. Especially the elderly. When they pass it is the thing that people most often regret - that they didn't pick up the phone, go for a drive, hold their loved one's hand or listen to their stories. Give them the precious gift of your time and in return they will give you precious memories to hold onto.

Advice

Advice is a funny fickle thing!
What was right for you in the past may not be right for you now. Just as other people's advice may have been right for them and the time and in the circumstances, they needed it. Listen to others advice with an open mind but chose the advice or path that feels right for you.

You know you best!

Heather

And finally, it all comes to an end (at the Surf Club, no less)

Facebook prompted me to add a Legacy Contact. This is someone who will manage, and I guess, close my Facebook account after I die. I did as requested and nominated one of my children. Facebook sent them an automated message that read:

"Hi …., Facebook lets people choose a legacy contact to manage their profile if something happens to them. As you know me well and I trust you, I chose you. Please let me know if you want to talk about this."

My clever child replied immediately with this response…

"I'll do one better, just sent it to post the following when you die…

Oi, we'll be having a bit of a gatho at 5pm Saturday at the Surf Club. Bar tab is local beer and house wines, if you want spirits buy them yourself. +1's welcome just let us know. Oh, and mum (Kellie) died, so dress code is dark colours. Gifts not required but certainly encouraged. Chuck us a like to let us know you're coming and comment for a +1, Cheers."

This made me laugh harder than it should have. ☺

Kellie M Cox

NOT THE END BUT JUST THE BEGINNING... UNTIL WE DO THIS AGAIN

I hope this book has inspired, has evoked emotions, because emotions are not our enemy. We need to feel the lows to feel the highs.

I even hope that you reach out to one of the contributors to share how their story has touched you, but obviously not in a stalkerish kind of a way, of course.

I hope you enjoy a full life, and when death does come, because she is like that and won't forget a single soul. When she does come, I hope your life has granted you memories and loved ones. These are the only two things that really matter and the only two things you will take with you.

So apparently the end isn't all that bad. You all get to come together at a surf club once more, have a wine or beer, just don't forget those presents that are certainly encouraged. What you bring to a funeral I have no idea. I guess my kids would appreciate gift cards, cash or bitcoins.

Life is only as serious as you make it but make you sure don't waste a moment doing anything that doesn't make your life amazing.

Until we do this again at sixty or even earlier, keep making memories with loved ones. I look forward to more contributions in a decade or less.

What we have created together in this book is magnificent. It is moving, it is wise. It is uniquely each and every one of you. I hope we can do it all over again for Book Two!

As a parting gift, I have included a chapter from my latest novel, The Last First Kiss. It is a sexy little chapter where the soulmates find each other again. This book is as close to a memoir as I will ever write. I began it in Rome back in 2015. I was travelling through Europe on my own for two months and meeting along the way absolutely incredible people. I had the beginning and end of the story in my mind but stopped writing it as I got a bit scared. The ending was not going to be a pleasant one and as I was journeying, parts of the story began happening. As in, I would write a character who suddenly appeared, or I would write a conversation that then occurred. The book sat for a few years before I had the courage to pick it up again and finish it in 2020.

The elevator pitch is two soulmates exploring the globe, romancing the cities we dream to visit and answering the age-old questions of life, love and death. There are certain parts of the story that actually occurred, as in the spiritual taxi driver who had an amazing story to tell, the wonderful landlord who rented me her beautiful home in Paris and the many conversations about soulmates with complete strangers who became friends. I hope you enjoy the chapter and the sneak peek at my latest work of fiction.

I will leave my final offering here, to inspire you all to continue to create. When you see my light on at three in the morning know I am writing and thinking of you creating too! Each and every one of you have become my magical muses.

***

Three in the morning, the time for writers, lovers and poets. Warm bodies huddle as their minds begin to awaken but unable or unwilling to concede to slumber once more, they take to their parchments.

Their words flow as their souls yearn to connect.

Magical muses inspiring in the dark still of the night.

Kellie M Cox

ACKNOWLEDGEMENTS

How do I acknowledge all the amazing people who were part of this project?

A heartfelt thank you to all my talented and inspiring friends who shared their journeys of sorrow, joy, learnings and great wisdom with me. I hope this is a book you can be proud to share with your family and friends.

My amazing team of Nadine Meyn, Elloise Sullivan, Blair Renwick and Connor Renwick who brought this book to life. This is the fifth book you have created in just three years. I will never be able to say thank you enough. I am in debt to you all forever. Love you all to bits!

As always are the dynamic duo of Melissa Spilsted and Mark P Simmons who have the first read of everything I write. Your guidance and excessive use of emojis when describing the manuscripts make me smile.

This has been a moving project and I would recommend anyone thinking of doing something similar to do so. Even, if you don't publish. The journey of creating this collection of wisdom has been inspiring.

A sneak peek at the novel, **THE LAST FIRST KISS** by Kellie M Cox

CHAPTER THREE

The Cemetery of the Capuchins, Rome, Italy

The tour continued and as Samantha stood in the fourth chapel of The Cemetery of the Capuchins, she was overwhelmed once more. This time by the thousands of bone fragments that decorated the walls, roof and corridor with thoughtful precision and calculation. The floor of the Chapel itself covered in dirt from Israel said to possess amazing powers of preservation. David told the story of a bouquet of flowers placed on the dirt remaining alive and preserved for weeks.

There was believed to be the remains of three thousand, seven hundred bodies in the tiny chapels located beneath the church. Thousands of bones adorned every available space before them; femurs, humeri, fibulas, scapulae and clavicles but mainly skulls. This was, after all nicknamed the skull chapel. They were told that current law prohibits human remains to be placed as displays of this kind, so if a single bone was to fall it must be afforded a proper burial. This would not be the first burial these remains had borne witness to but it would be their last.

At the centre of the impressive commemoration, two arms crossed in solidarity, said to represent both man and Christ and symbolise that they are one in the same. Both man - both vulnerable. The imagined faces of the hundreds of skulls staring back at the group spoke to each of the tourists. The impermanence of life, the certainty of death for each of the wide-eyed travellers in plain view for them all as a reminder of their own predetermined fate.

The room held the group in awe. Not only, of the hundreds of souls lost, but at the mastery of the artwork. The skulls once hidden behind the face of mortal man now lined neatly against the plastered wall of the ancient church. Row after row of the human skeletons placed with care to form intricate patterns in the decorative chapel. In the corners and at either side of the room, the garment of the Capuchin friars stood, arms folded in front. Their skulls holding in place the hood of the worn garment. Small crosses stood positioned in the ground below. The inscriptions of the sacred placements weathered by time. The small chapel was a transparent reminder of the swift passage of life and one's mortality.

The group ventured further down the corridor as David asked another question that few from the group seemed to be able to answer.

"What do you notice about this clock?"

The group was quiet until the attentive mother from London spoke, "It has no hands."

It seemed a strange answer given that the clock that sat majestically before them was made up entirely of finger bones and vertebrae.

The group stared at the clock on the wall. The indicators of time measuring to VI each formed with carefully placed finger bones nailed to the wall behind them. The outer rim of the circular piece was adorned by vertebrae, inside which more bones were placed to create an inner sphere.

David continued, "And what do you think is the meaning behind the clock?"

The visiting mother spoke again, obviously pleased to have made the connection, "It means time can't be controlled."

Samantha nodded her head in agreement. This message was becoming clearer and clearer as she made her way through Italy. Time flies. Time waits for no man. You can't turn back the hands of time. How many different ways did she need to hear the same message and yet what had she done for most of her life. She had wasted the most precious commodity she had been given - time.

David instructed the group to move to the final chapel. "Come forward everyone. I want everyone to get a good look at this one. Come on, squash up. We are all friends here now. Sam, move a little closer up this way."

David placed his hand around Samantha and maneuvered her closer to him. The group was silent as David once more told of the history of the monks' remains displayed prominently before them. "Now, do you remember what we said before about time?" he asked. The group hummed in agreement as if entranced by his words as they waited for him to continue.

"So, remember what the message here is. It's about time and this is what this final chapel represents to me. We bring you here not to feel any fear for what is displayed, not to feel any sadness for the people whose lives are now over. Instead, this journey tonight is about time and making sure we use our time wisely. Death is the ultimate leveller- none of us can control it and none of us can afford to waste the precious days we have been given to live our lives."

The group was thoughtful as they stood, some holding tightly the wrought iron black bars that separated themselves from the bones of the thousands of monks before them. Every one of the tour group was taking their individual time to absorb his words and the messages within them. Eyes darted from left to right, from the floor to the ceiling. Samantha herself tried to take in every inch of the scene before her, knowing one day it would just be her memory of this image alone that she would need to rely on.

Samantha felt David's presence close. He had barely moved more than a couple of feet from her for the entire time they had been in the narrow corridor that displayed the monks' remains. She felt the warmth of David's chest against her back. She felt once more his hand on her.

David pulled Samantha in closer. He leant down and whispered into her ear. "Hanoi… The Temple of the Horse."

Samantha knew instantly what those words meant. That was how she recognised David. She had seen him in Vietnam, about a year or so earlier, inside The Temple of the Horse. The temple was a stunning little chapel located down a small alleyway in the Old Quarter of the dusty streets of Hanoi, Vietnam.

"That was you!" she smiled as the mystery unfolded.

"And that was you!" he smiled back.

Without taking a pause, he addressed the group again, "And that my good people, is the end of our tour tonight. I will give you a chance to have a look through the bookshop and I will be on the stairs outside to answer any final questions you might have. Take your time."

David looked down once more into Samantha's eyes, "See you outside beautiful," he toyed with her.

Samantha felt her body shake as she once again found a quiet place to still her mind. Hanoi. Of course, she thought to herself. She remembered the day well, she had thought about it often, the day she nearly met the dark-haired stranger in The Temple of the Horse. In Vietnam it is custom for temples to have a theme or main point of interest and she just happened to walk into The Temple of the Horse one day while getting lost in the Old Quarter of Hanoi.

The temple was one that didn't allow photos, which meant Samantha stood in silence taking it all in. She walked into the main temple and found the most elegant statue of a grey horse she had ever seen. The horse had eyelashes; long eyelashes that made its eyes pop and gave them life. The horse brought back lovely memories of the father she had lost years earlier. In that moment she lowered her head in prayer to honour her beloved parent.

As she closed her eyes, she remembered the loving, caring man that was her father. She spoke to him, quietly telling him she loved him, when she was suddenly startled by someone close by to her. She looked over and caught the eyes of a stranger staring back at her. Feeling slightly teary at the loss of the father she loved so much, she made her way to the door for some fresh air. Not that the air was in any way refreshing at that time of the year in Hanoi. The temperatures had been constantly hitting a high and humid thirty-six to thirty-eight degrees every day.

Sitting down on the front steps of the temple, she allowed a few light tears to flow. Once upon a time there would have been no stopping the tears from flowing freely at the memory of what she had lost, but over time she was able to control the sadness behind the grief to focus more and more on the loving memories that she carried in her heart of her beloved father.

She looked up again and the stranger was in front of her. She saw him walk toward her and then turn suddenly. She wondered if he was going to ask for directions and she tried her hardest to pull herself together. She realised she didn't look her most respectable at that present point in time. Sitting on a step in the dirt, shoes still removed as is respectful in the temple, tears rolling down her face, sniffling slightly, sweating profusely, she glanced up at the stranger. His amazing eyes bore down on her. He appeared to want to say something. She nearly spoke a word of greeting to him. He opened his mouth and then turned again.

Samantha looked down into her bag to find a tissue. She took a moment to gather herself before standing, ready to leave the temple grounds. She glanced around momentarily for the handsome stranger with the piercing eyes but he was gone. She had thought often about that day. It was obvious the stranger had wanted to say something. She didn't know what, and she regretted never finding out. And now, only twelve months later, here he was in Rome.

Samantha felt empowered. She headed to the bookstore after the tour, which was not something she wouldn't ever normally do. She purchased two postcards to remind her of the astounding images she had seen but had been unable to photograph due to the tight restrictions protecting the remains against photography.

She stood in line behind a young family from Dubai and watched as the father tried on bracelets. When it was her turn at the counter, she asked to see one of the bracelets, a series of small black skulls joined by a sturdy piece of black string. Yes, this was what she needed; a reminder, a constant reminder of how precious time was.

She made her purchase and headed outside into the cold night air to hear David's final words of wisdom for Rome. She couldn't wait and took the bracelet out of the packet and placed it on her left wrist. As she turned each skull over she saw the slight imperfections of each one. A large crack in the top of one, a deformed eye socket in another. Just amazing, she thought to herself, another reminder of the imperfect beauty of the human form.

"Sam?" David startled her from her daydream. "Are you ok?" His final speech was over.

"Yes, just lost in my thoughts," she reassured him.

"Did you enjoy the tour of the crypts and the catacombs?"

She stopped and thought before answering honestly. "Yes, it has given me a lot to think about."

"Sam… do you remember?" His words were quiet and hopeful. He was referring once more to their near meeting in Hanoi.

"Yes absolutely. I was a crying, dirty, sweaty mess on the step of the temple and you were going to speak to me."

"I wanted to but I saw that you were upset so I wanted to give you a couple of minutes and then I turned around and you were gone. I walked up and down the street looking for you. I had hoped to see you again in Vietnam. I looked out for you everywhere I went."
Samantha laughed and the more she laughed the harder she laughed. David joined her; the relief for him was immense. He was grateful that she remembered him as well.

"David, I searched everywhere I went for you as well. How insane is that?" She touched his face lightly. "You didn't have the beard back then. You looked very different."

"Vietnam was far too hot to wear this thing," he replied as he scratched his dark beard with his thumb and his forefinger. He was thoughtful for a moment as he stared directly into her hopeful eyes.

"Sam, this is the sanest thing that has ever happened to me." He reached down and cupped her chin. "I am going to kiss you now before you have a chance to run away again."

He lowered his head and placed his mouth on hers. Samantha reached around his waist and held him tightly. Nothing had felt more comfortable or more right to her in her entire life before. Their kiss was slow and heartfelt. His lips delicately skimmed over her sensitive skin. His tongue flirted with her lips before finding her welcoming mouth.

Samantha allowed every ounce of her being to relax and melt into the moment. Her body was limp but at the same time electric and alive. She relaxed and enjoyed the feeling of every single sensation.

"David? Excuse me?" The male American accent broke through their moment of passion.

David paused and sighed as he pulled his mouth away from Samantha's. "I won't be a moment. Don't go anywhere!" he warned her.

David walked toward the last remaining tour guest, obviously lost and feeling helpless in the massive city, he needed help with directions from his experienced guide.

Samantha felt for the cold stone pillar behind her for support. She traced her bottom lip with her tongue to taste David once more. She felt alive but so very calm. She had once read that when you meet your soulmate, there wouldn't be fireworks or instant passion and lust but instead an intense feeling of calm and peace.

"Soulmate," she laughed to herself. There she was getting ahead of herself again. It was one kiss. Just one kiss she had to remind herself.

David returned to her side, "Let's get out of here."

Without waiting for a response, he once again took Samantha's hand and walked her down the stairs of the magnificent church. He stopped halfway, turned to her and kissed her once more. This time the passion and lust were undeniable. His breath was warm and his mouth sweet. Samantha could feel her new bracelet on her wrist. The small black skulls reminding her that time is short.

"David," she stopped him, "I am renting a loft just a street away. Will you come back with me?"

He looked down at her and smiled. "I thought you would never ask," he teased her.

Neither of the two will ever remember the few moments it took to walk to the loft. Instead, both anticipating what was to come, they walked quickly and with purpose. They strode to the loft in a dream-like state, both grinning, both silent as their minds raced with endless possibilities.

They climbed the narrow spiral staircase to the small quiet loft in the centre of Rome. The room was hot from the timed heating that was working its magic, so Samantha opened the door to the small terrace for two. The cool breeze through the door was a relief as the heat of their bodies once more joined and grew exponentially.

They removed their jackets, which were soon discarded on the floor. Samantha wasted no time and began to tug at David's jumper. He released it without a fight. He pulled Samantha's scarf above her head and began unbuttoning her jeans. She skillfully kicked off her boots and worked quickly on removing his t-shirt before starting on the zipper of his pants.

Clothes were falling to the ground, layers upon layers of unraveling, like a delicious, decadent desert. David stopped. "Sam, are you sure this is what you want?"

Samantha lifted her left wrist to display the symbol of time to him. "I am not wasting a mere second more thinking about how much I want this."

With that, David lifted her legs around his waist and carried her to the bed. With just a thin layer of material separating them, he removed the last shred of her clothing to stand for a moment and take in the beauty of the woman before him. He licked his lips again. He removed his final piece of clothing and lay down next to Samantha. For a moment, she was fearful that he didn't want to continue.

"What is it?" she begged of him.

"I just can't believe this is happening. That you are here."

She imagined she could almost see tears well in his eyes. "David... make love to me." Her words were pleading, lustful and without patience.

David rolled toward her and immediately joined with her. There was no time to waste. They needed to feel their bodies join. They craved to feel as close as two people could feel.

* * *

Samantha woke in his arms. The cold air from the open terrace door stirred through the room but couldn't penetrate the warm and protective capsule they had formed together. She rolled over to face him and stared at her sleeping David. He stirred ever so slightly, and she kissed his lips. His eyes fluttered open and his immediate smile shined through the darkened room.

"I didn't just dream it then?" he asked her. She kissed him again.

"Shh... go back to sleep now." She snuggled into his chest and closed her eyes. She couldn't ever remember a time she felt so right about anything before. She planted one final kiss on his bare chest and fell into a peaceful slumber.